The Life and Times of an Ordinary Joe Named John

by
John K. Silberman

PublishAmerica

Baltimore

First printing

ISBN: 1-4137-1291-6
PUBLISHED BY PUBLISHAMERICA, LLLP
www.publishamerica.com
Baltimore

Printed in the United States of America

To my wife Barbara, "Bobbie", who has made The Life and Times of an Ordinary Joe named John worth living

****

To my children Ann, Tracy, and Patrick who make me proud!

Table of Contents

Preface

September 27, 2002

Notice of Termination

John Silberman
504 S. Minnesota Street
Carson City, Nevada 89703

Dear John:

This letter is to confirm our discussion today regarding your employment separation from MSX International. Our current business performance requires that we take action to reduce our operating costs and reorganize specific operations. With regret, I must inform you that your position is being eliminated effective September 30, 2002.

Sincerely,

(Signed)

Derek Grills
Senior Vice President
Human Capital Management Services

Although I had been expecting this letter, it still was a shock to receive it and I realized that I had been terminated for no good reason. I have included this letter as both a start and finish to my memoirs. The main focus in this book will be on the events that took place in my business career. If I have another book left in me, it will explore more important matters such as my family and friends. But I have to get started on this one, and here's how it happened.

"Goddamn it, dear. This bastard has been trying to get rid of me for over a year and he finally succeeded."

"Well, John, you shouldn't be so surprised. We saw it coming. They haven't even been subtle about how, at your age, you don't fit into their organization. They were smart enough to set you up so it would be hard for you to sue them for age discrimination."

"Yeah, but what the hell am I going to do now? I've been working for over fifty years, I have no hobbies, and since my back went out I can't even play sports anymore."

"Well, you know, you've been telling me stories all of our married life about your experiences in boarding school, college, and the military. Why don't you write a book about your life and that way you'll have something to do that will keep you busy, and out of my kitchen?"

"Hell, dear, you know the only things I have ever written were business memos and reports. I don't have a clue as how to write a story, much less a book. Where do I begin?"

"John, I suggest that you start at the beginning."

"What the hell is the beginning? Oh well! I'll try and see what happens."

The first real memories that I have began at age eleven when I started school in the 7th grade at Bordentown Military Institute, located in Bordentown, New Jersey. I had been going to grade school at Hunter Elementary in New York City till the 6th grade. Hunter decided that they would no longer have boys in the classes from the seventh grade and higher. My parents, who were divorced at the time, had to make a decision as to where I was to continue my education and they decided on B.M.I.

"Johnny, how would you like to have a nice military uniform and go away to a boarding school?"

"Gee, Mom, I'll miss you, Patsy, Hiwa, and Rhythm."

"Oh, you'll get to come home often, and it will be just like when you went off to camp in the summers."

"Please Mom, don't send me away! I promise I'll be a good boy!"

As an adult, I wondered how anyone in their right mind could send an eleven-year-old kid away from home, and to a military school, no less. I thought I must have been a terrible brat who was always in some kind of trouble. The truth of the matter, I learned later, was that I was an obstacle to my mother's pursuit of happiness with her various boyfriends. My dad, who was a brilliant businessman and who was also a playboy, had a buddy by the name of Eddie Davis who was the co-owner of a nightclub on 52nd street in New York. "Leon and Eddie's" was a popular nightspot famous for sponsoring musicians such as Miles Davis and Dizzy Gillespie. Eddie Davis's son was attending B.M.I., and that's how it was decided that I should be sent to Bordentown to continue my education. Not too much thought was given to that decision, but it was a convenient solution for my parents, and for me, it was probably the defining moment in my life.

Chapter One
Pre-Bordentown Military Institute

I don't have a whole lot of memories of my life before going off to boarding school; I can only guess that I was not a happy little boy and that I probably suppressed many memories because they were not especially pleasant.

Of the things that I do remember are some of the places that I lived in in Manhattan. One of my first memories is living in a luxurious duplex in the Fifth Avenue Hotel with my sister Patsy, my nanny Hilda (Hiwa), and my mom and dad, who were still married at that time, but barely.

"Dave, where the hell were you last night and how come you didn't come home?

"Sibyl, if I had somebody to come home to, I would."

"What? Were you out with your whore of a girlfriend again?"

"Shut the fuck up Sibyl, the children can hear us."

I must have been about six because they were divorced when I was seven years old. A duplex apartment in New York City consisted of two floors with the living room, kitchen, and dining room downstairs and the bedrooms on the upper floor. One of my memories was sitting on the stairs with my sister Patsy, who was four and a half years older than I. We were watching my mother and father take a little red fire truck that had pedals on it out of a box and place it under the Christmas tree.

"See all those presents, Johnny? Mom and Dad bought those for us. There is no Santa Claus, Johnny, and he doesn't bring us any presents. Stop crying, Johnny!" The first of life's many disillusionments.

While living at the hotel, I vaguely recall taking two trips to Europe on the passenger ship *Normandy*. My father had become very rich and was know as the "Zipper King" for his many patents and inventions of machinery that made zippers. My mother, Sibyl Reder, and my father, David Silberman, were married in 1925. My mother was my father's bookkeeper until they struck it rich and started traveling to Europe.

My mother rented a villa in Cannes and we spent the summers living on the French Riviera. She started to hobnob with the likes of Lord and Lady Chamberlin and Giovanni Martinelli, the famed Metropolitan Opera tenor. I don't recall many of the events that took place while living in France but I do know that my sister and I became fluent in the French language and were bilingual at that time. I believe that while my mother was experiencing life in the international jet set (in the days before jets), my Dad fell in love with an Irish lass, Ida Raffloer, and subsequently married her. She converted to Judaism as insisted upon by my dad's parents, my grandparents, who were Orthodox Jews.

Years later, at my father's request, my Irish fiancée, Barbara Birmingham, agreed to let him introduce her to his parents "as a nice Jewish girl from Brownsville." My grandparents did not buy it for one second, and when we married in the Catholic Church, they sat Shiva for me. (A prayer for the dead.) They were such good Jews that they never took the opportunity of meeting their great grandkids much to the heartbreak of my father who loved our children very much.

On the second trip back from Europe, two new personalities entered my life. My mother had acquired a Wirehaired terrier named Rhythm who was the cutest little dog that my sister and I adored to pieces. We had Rhythm through many different homes until I went to Bordentown when my mother gave her to my uncle Milton, my dad's brother.

The second new personality that entered my life was my beloved Hiwa, Hilda Cordice, who my mother hired to be our nanny, maid, cook, and housekeeper. In reality, she became our mother as she loved my sister and me unconditionally and we loved her back. She was part of our lives and our children's lives until she died from cancer while living with my sister. She was one of the three mothers that I had while growing up and into my adult years. I had my birth mother, Sibyl. I had Hilda, and I had my step-mom, Ida, who I adored until her passing on March 1, 2002, at the ripe old age of 89.

While living at the Fifth Avenue Hotel, my parents separated and Hiwa took on the responsibility of being our mom since my dad was living with Ida and my mom was cavorting around with lots of boyfriends, many of whom were famous theatrical people. Finally, in April 1938 my mother sued for divorce on the only grounds available in those days, which was infidelity. The proceeding got quite ugly as my mother accused my father of getting a Mexican divorce and marrying Ida whereas my dad accused my mother of sleeping around with the likes of Sir Warden Chilcott, a famous British naval expert, and many others including the famous tenor. The divorce was granted and my mother was given custody of my sister and me with my father having visiting rights on weekends, with the express proviso that we were not allowed to visit with Ida. My mother had asked for $150.00 a week in alimony but the judge only granted her $34.00 because at that time she was the owner of a salon called the Sylph Shop located in the Hotel Navarre. Her brother-in-law, Dr. Simon Ruskin, had provided her with the capital to establish the salon that soon failed because of her lack of business experience.

Shortly after the divorce, my dad became broke, which he periodically did over his lifetime, because he was a compulsive gambler. My dad made millions many times over in his life, but the bookies always wound up with the cash. He just could not stand prosperity.

Now with my dad broke and my mom's business a failure it was time to move from the Fifth Avenue Hotel and out of the life of luxury. My mom's brother-in-law, Dr.Simon Ruskin, was a very wealthy man who was a saint. In addition to being a physician, he was a scientist who developed a form of penicillin, which reaped him a fortune. He had a five-story house located at 32 East 67th Street in which his crazy wife, Francis (Sibyl's sister) his three children, Asa, Carol and Arianne, his mother-in-law (my grandmother) Anne, and my great uncle Joe (my grandmother's brother) all lived.

He took my mother, my sister, Rhythm, and Hilda under his roof and housed us and fed us. There is much about this period of time that I have suppressed. I know my sister and I were miserable, as was my mother. We were made to know the charity that was being provided to us on a daily basis by my horrible Aunt Francis.

Living with the Ruskins was not all bad. My cousin Asa was a few years older than I was. We became pals and we had a lot of fun playing together. My sister Pat and Carole also became friends and did a lot of girl stuff together. I remember Hiwa taking Asa and me to Central Park where we would sail little boats on Walden Pond

"Asa, you and Johnny be careful and don't fall in the water!"

"Oh. Hiwa, we know better than that!"

On other occasions Hiwa would take us to the Park and march behind us while we would give out literature for my Aunt Francis' run for Congress.

"Don't you boys talk to any strangers. You just give out those papers and don't talk to any one."

"Oh, Hiwa, we know better than that!" Fortunately for the country, and us, my Aunt Francis was not elected to Congress.

On Sundays, Asa and I were required to go to Temple Emmanuel in order to learn Hebrew and become familiar with Jewish culture. Since the temple was a short walk from the Ruskin's house, we were permitted to walk there by ourselves without Hilda tagging along behind us. We were each given a quarter which was to go to the fund for the establishment of the Jewish State in Palestine.

"Hey, Johnny, let's go to the candy store and buy some candy."

" Sir, can I have two boxes of Goobers (chocolate covered peanuts) and one box of Raisinets (chocolate covered raisins)?"

I'm not sure what Asa bought but all I know is the fund only got a dime from each of us. That probably explains why it took so long for the creation of the Jewish State of Israel. However, we had candy all through the Hebrew lessons.

Asa was more adventuresome than I was. I remember one summer when we were at the Ruskin's summer vacation home in Nyack, New York, Asa put his hand in the wringer of the washing machine and turned the switch on to see what would happen. Well, naturally the wringer started to eat my cousin's arm and luckily, Hiwa, who was never far away, saw what was going on and pulled the plug. Her speedy action probably saved Asa's arm from being broken.

As rich as the Ruskins were, my Aunt Francis was a tightwad. I remember her spanking Asa one day because he had accidentally broken a light bulb that cost about a nickel. Having dinner with the Ruskins was a nightmare that I will never forget. They had a large dining room and the entire family was required to eat together, both adults and children. Most of the times, Uncle Simon would be absent, either taking care of some patient, or being creative in his lab that was located in the basement of the house. That would leave Francis in charge and God forbid that any of us children would leave anything uneaten on our plates that the starving children in China would love to have. We would either have to eat whatever it was that we did not like or forfeit dessert. Another part of the dinner ritual was that one of us children would have to speak on a subject that my Aunt Francis would select and the other children would have to comment on our presentation.

"Johnny, what did President Roosevelt mean when he said, 'The only thing we have to fear is fear itself.'?"

"I don't know, Aunt Francis."

"You may be excused from the dinner table and you will go straight to your room and think about the answer to my question!"

My grandmother, Anna, was a nice old lady who used to make crullers and mint iced tea in the summertime at the Ruskin's home in Nyack. She didn't have much to say to us boys but I can recall her yakking away in Yiddish with my mother and Aunt Francis. I don't know what they were talking about but the name David came up frequently. I guess they were badmouthing my dad who I think was living with Ida in Florida at that time recovering from some type of circulation problem. One night Asa and I were eavesdropping on a conversation that my aunt and uncle were having.

"Francis," Simon said. "How much longer are we going to have to take care of Dave Silberman's brats?"

"I don't know. Probably as long as it takes for that bastard to stop gambling and start making money again."

This was the only time I heard anything negative concerning me come out of my uncle's mouth. Although I was stung by my uncle's comments, which I was not supposed to hear, I think my cousin Asa was more upset than I was. Asa, later in life, became a doctor after attending medical school in France where he married a lovely French girl. He became head of a big hospital in the Bronx, New York, and unfortunately died of an aneurism at a relatively early age.

We lived with the Ruskins for about two years before my father started to make one of his frequent trips to the millionaire's club via a new zipper business. He started to pay my mother alimony again, and she also found a job in a department store as a sales clerk in the linen department. She was able to move Hilda, my sister, and our dog Rhythm, and herself to a cute little apartment at 225 East 74th Street in Manhattan. What she wasn't able to take with her was the expensive furniture that she had moved from the Fifth Avenue Hotel when we began to live with the Ruskins. I think Francis considered the furniture as payment for having to take care of the Silberman brats for as long as she did. The furniture was a bone of contention between the two sisters over many years but my mother never got her belongings back.

The apartment was numbered 1P which meant it was on the first floor so we did not have to use the elevator to go from our apartment to the 74th Street entrance. My dad started to exercise his weekend rights to visit with us kids and he would pick us up in a taxi in front of the apartment house.

"Dave, you have those children back here by 5p.m. and not one minute later!"

He would frequently take my sister and me to a movie and then up to his apartment where we would visit with his wife, Ida, despite the fact that there was a court order prohibiting him from doing so. I knew my mom was wise to this.

"If you kids see your father's whore of a wife, do not eat any candy that she may offer you because it is poisoned!"

Can you imagine offering little kids candy and having them refuse it? Ida must have thought we didn't like the stuff because we never let her know that our mother said she was trying to poison us. Ida was not only beautiful physically but she was a beautiful person. She would make lunches and early dinners for Pat and myself that were delicious and since there was no prohibition about eating meals we would gobble them down. My mother couldn't cook and Hilda was a marginal cook at best, so Ida's meals were always a treat. I remember several occasions when my dad would get us back late, and my mother would be waiting in front of the apartment building.

"Dave," she would scream "I told you to have these children back by 5p.m. and its now 5:30. If you want these kids to visit you in the future, you better do what I tell you!"

"Yes, Sibyl."

I can't imagine that it was much fun for him to visit with his children when he would be faced with that kind of abuse at the end of the day.

After living in apartment 1P for about six months, a larger apartment became available on the 5th floor and so we moved once again, this time to apartment 5P. This is how I met my first girlfriend, Nancy. She lived with her mom and dad on the 7th floor. One day while I was waiting by the elevator door so that I could take Rhythm for her afternoon walk, the elevator door opened and inside was the cutest little girl with pigtails and freckles across her nose. She had a little bulldog with her.

"Hi, what's your dog's name?"

"His name is Samson and I'm Nancy."

"Hello, Nancy. My name's Johnny and this is my dog Rhythm."

Our dogs took one look at each other and decided to be friendly.

Nancy and I took one look at each other and also decided to become fast friends. To this day, I remember her phone number. Back then telephone numbers were not all digits. The first two digits were alpha, followed by five numeric digits. In the area that we lived in the first two digits were RH that stood for Rhinelander. So Nancy's phone number was RH 4 1493. I made up a little saying to help me memorize Nancy's number. "1492 Columbus sailed the ocean blue, 1493, Nancy loves me." Pretty slick for a nine-year-old boy.

Nancy and I became inseparable except when I was playing with my little street boy friends. Although she was somewhat of a tomboy, we guys would never consider letting a girl in on the games we played in the streets of New York City. Nancy and I would walk our dogs together twice a day and on weekends we would go to the movies at Lowe's at 72nd Street on Lexington Avenue. Hilda or my sister would always escort us to the movies and pick us up once the show was over. Occasionally, my sister would join us but not too often, because she hated sitting in the children's section, which was policed by a matron who always dressed in what looked like a nurse's uniform. For eleven cents we would get a double feature, two cartoons, the news, and one episode of a serial movie such as *Sheena, Queen of the Jungle*. I always complained about having to have Hilda escort us. I thought I was a big enough boy to take my girlfriend to the movies without a nanny trailing behind. I was always overruled.

Nancy and I enjoyed talking to each other on the telephone when we got home from school.

"Hi, Nancy, this is Johnny. Would you like to go to the movies this Saturday? There is a great double feature starring Tom Mix."

"Sure, Johnny, I'd love to, but do we have to have Hiwa tagging along?"

"I'll ask her if we can go by ourselves, but I doubt it."

"Johnny, have you ever kissed anyone?"

"Never, but I'd like to kiss you, if you'd let me."

"Maybe, at the movie, if your sister doesn't come with us."

"Wow, Nancy!"

Using the phone was OK until my mother came home from work

at which time the telephone became her exclusive property. My sister and I were not allowed to use it in case she would miss out on one of her "important" calls. To get around this, I devised a private phone system that Nancy and I used. The system consisted of two Dixie cups connected by a piece of string. Nancy's apartment was two stories above mine and she would lower one of the Dixie cups from her window and I would catch it when it dangled in front of my window. We could then speak to each other by taking turns talking into the Dixie cup and then putting the cup to an ear to listen. When we tired of talking we would pass secret written messages back and forth using one of the cups as the messenger.

It became fashionable and more prestigious at this time for kids to have white nannies. Hilda, who was born in Barbados, was a colored lady with the emphasis on lady. For her entire life she considered herself colored, never black, never African-American or whatever became the popular terminology for Negroes. Well, my mother fired Hiwa despite the fact that Hiwa worked without pay during those tortuous years we were living with the Ruskins. The only reason that she worked under those conditions was that she loved my sister and I so much that she wanted to act as a buffer between my crazy Aunt Francis and us. Regardless, my mother had to be socially correct so despite Hiwa's loyalty, she was let go and replaced with a young white girl, Sandy.

I woke up one morning with a horrible stomach ache that turned out to be an attack of appendicitis. I was rushed to the hospital where Dr. Ritter performed an emergency appendectomy. The only anesthesia available then was ether. It was administered by placing a cone over your nose and allowing the ether to drop until you became unconscious. It was like being smothered to death. As I was going under, I must have lashed out because I hit Dr. Ritter a good one and gave him a black eye. He got even with me later. Before I was ready to go home he slipped a pair of closed scissors under the clamps that held the wound together and opened them till the clamp popped out. I screamed at Dr. Ritter to stop it. He slapped me across the face which made me shut up and also revenged the shiner that I had given him.

While I was in the hospital, recovering from the surgery, Sandy took my sister to the park to play. This was the same park that Hiwa used to take us to. I would play on the monkey bars and my sister would play on the swings. Lo and behold, this day Hiwa was sitting on a park bench and asked my sister how I was. She did not know that I had gone to the hospital for surgery but she had a premonition that I was sick. Hiwa walked back to the apartment with Sandy and my sister. My mother fired Sandy on the spot and rehired Hiwa. My mother accused Sandy of stealing. She showed how she had put a pencil mark at the top of the fluid level of an opened bottle of booze. The level of the booze was below where she had marked the bottle, and therefore Sandy had stolen some of my mother's precious liquor. This was a lesson well learned. When I was older (about fourteen) I would drink my mother's booze and then fill up the bottle with water until the level reached her pencil mark. I wonder if her guests ever complained about the watered down drinks they were served.

As my dad started to accumulate big bucks again, he would include me, along with his other buddies, on jaunts to major sporting events. My dad never learned how to drive, but he always had some kind of prestigious car and a chauffeur to drive him around. One of the chauffeurs that I remember vividly was a fellow by the name of Lew Staff who acted as my father's major gofer guy as well as his driver. Lew taught me how to box and was the fellow who first drove me to Bordentown. At any rate, my dad loved sports and especially boxing. He had boxed in the navy under the name of Pete Silburn and was the lightweight fleet champion.

My dad took me to watch Joe Louis fight on several occasions and we always had ringside seats. Many of his buddies would come to the fights with us. Among them were fellows like Canadian Lee, a heavyweight contender, Jimmy Walker, the Mayor of NYC, Three-Finger Brown, a mafia hood, and other assorted and colorful characters. The bookies would come over and pay their respects and collect their money. My dad bet on every sporting event that we ever attended and more often than not wound up on the losing side of the bet.

One of my dad's favorite things was the "Sport of Kings", horse racing. On Saturdays in the summertime, he would gather up his cronies and take me with them either to Aqueduct or Belmont racetrack. There were always eight races. My dad would give me $16.00 so I could bet two bucks on each race. Naturally, the tellers would not accept bets from a kid so I would wind up the day with sixteen dollars in my pockets. Dad, on the other hand, would bet hundreds of dollars on each race and would end his day with the bookies having a lot more money than they started with. This never seemed to bother him as he and his buddies would be telling jokes and kidding about their affairs with various girlfriends. Although I was just a little guy, they treated me as one of their own. To tell the truth, I really did not understand much of what they were talking about but when they all started to laugh at the punch line to some dirty joke, I would join them in laughter although I did not have a clue as to what the joke was all about. After the races Dad would take me back to my apartment where I would share my "winnings" with my sister, as she, being a girl, was not permitted to go to the track with us guys.

Dad also loved baseball. Once in a while, on a Sunday, we would go to Yankee Stadium to see a doubleheader. This was an experience that we shared together since he never invited his buddies along. I remember him teaching me how to score games and what the batting averages of his favorite players were. The part I liked best was the hot dogs and peanuts and the 7th inning stretch where he would let me take a sip of his beer. As a result of these outings, I developed a love for the game and became an ardent Brooklyn Dodger fan, much to the chagrin of my dad. I used to spend days on end sitting on a chair in my mother's apartment listening to Red Barber broadcast the Brooklyn Dodger games. His description of what was going on in the ballpark were more realistic in my mind than what I see when I watch a game on TV today. Although I was a Dodger fan, my dad never took me to Ebbets Field to watch them play. He always took me to Yankee Stadium to watch the Yankees; that was his team.

One of my mother's cousins, Harry Reder, was a part owner of a boy's camp, Camp Kohut, located in Poland, Maine. When I was six years old I was sent to this camp and my sister was sent to a girl-scout camp located in upstate New York. The summer camp lasted six weeks and after being homesick for a while I really got to enjoy what the camp had to offer. I learned how to swim in the lake that was adjacent to the camp property. On Saturdays, they would line us boys up by age group, and the camp nurse would make us jump in the lake, then soap each of us up individually, and have us jump back into the lake to rinse off. That was when I experienced my first hardon as the camp nurse seemed particularly interested in seeing that my genital area was well soaped up.

It was at this camp that I received my first tennis lesson and tennis became a passion of mine. I would play tennis all through high school, college, and into my adult years until my back went out in my early sixties. I became fairly proficient and played on the B.M.I. varsity squad but was not good enough to play on the Cornell team. As an adult, I played as a team member on several of the swim and tennis clubs that we belonged to. I was competitive as a C or D player but if I tried at a higher level, I could not win against another club's team member.

Another skill that I developed at camp was acting. We would put on shows once a week on Saturday nights and I always managed to have a role. I continued acting through high school and because of this background, I also participated in several forensic speaking contests. I even became the New Jersey forensic speaking champ in my junior year at B.M.I. I went to Camp Kohut for four straight years and I believe the camping experience helped me to adjust to life in a boarding school when I was sent to B.M.I at eleven years of age.

One of the requirements imposed on us campers, was that we had to write home at least once a week. Our counselors would read the letters before we sent them. If any complaints were made about the camp, they would censor the comments out, and make us rewrite the letters making sure we praised the food, the sports, and especially the counselors in charge of our tents. The counselors were paid a pittance for their duties and relied heavily on the tips that they received from our parents after we were returned home. They insisted that we had great things to say about them even if we really didn't like them at all.

In 1992 we had to put my mother in a nursing home as she was suffering from a severe case of Alzheimer's disease. When my wife, my sister and I went to clean out her apartment we came across a box that contained, among other things, the letters that I wrote her from camp Kohut all those many years ago.

When the camping season was over and before I had to go back to school, there were all kinds of games that we kids used to play in the streets and parks of New York City. I remember taking the subway to Van Courtland Park in the Bronx to play football as a team member of a group that I belonged to. On the way to the park we would thumb wrestle against each other. The game was played by joining my right hand with my opponent's right hand, and then attempt to pin his thumb against the side of his hand. In subsequent years I taught my children and my grandchildren this game, and when I felt they were old enough, I would let them win two out of three games against me and that would make them the champion of the thumb game.

When we arrived at the park, we would practice and be coached on how to play football. Occasionally, we would play a team from another group. There were no gangs backs then, just groups. A teacher or school principal led a group and its purpose was to give the kids something to do after school and on weekends. This was not free. My parents had to pay to have me belong to my group that was called Columbia, named after the college. At any rate, I was trained to be a running back because I was too small to play on the line and I could barely catch the football, so being a receiver was out of the question. I became quite proficient as a running back because I could run like the wind, especially if some big kid was trying to catch me and tackle me to the ground.

After the game or practice we would all get back on the subway for the trip back to Manhattan which took approximately an hour and a half from Van Courtland Park in the Bronx. The subway fare was a nickel. Now I think it is about $1.50. We were all hungry as hell after playing all afternoon and I would eat a sandwich and drink a carton of milk that Hiwa had prepared for me earlier that morning. After eating, most of us would doze off as we were rocked to sleep by the motion of the subway car and by being really tired and satisfied with food.

After school, on the days that I wasn't playing with Nancy or going to group, my buddies and I would amuse ourselves with a number of games that we would play in the street in front of my apartment building on East 74th street. Among my favorites was stickball. We would set up a baseball field with certain cars designated as first base, second base, etc. With a broom handle serving as a bat and a little pink Spalding ball we would enjoy a lively game of baseball with as few as two players or as many kids as were available. There wasn't much traffic back then so we could play several innings before being interrupted by a car coming through.

Another of my favorite street games was hockey, which we played on roller skates. We would buy hockey sticks and would wrap electrician's tape around the bottom of the sticks to protect them from splitting. For a puck we would use any little flat object that we could find but once in a while one of the kids would come up with a real puck and that would make the game more fun. These games would sometimes get out of hand with the hockey sticks being used to trip each other up. Many were the times I would go home with skinned knees and elbows but with a smile on my face if I had been successful in tripping up another kid.

My mother was always interested in the stock market. She had a lot of wealthy friends in the theatrical field and wisely decided that if she could become a stockbroker she would have some ready-made clients. She took several courses and did whatever was required of her to become a licensed stockbroker in New York State. As a matter of fact, she was one of the very first female stockbrokers ever. Her strategy worked and she was able to give up her job in the department store. She became a full-time broker; several wealthy people traded with her and the commissions started to roll in. Park Avenue (a prestigious location in New York) beckoned and she found apartment

5E., a two-bedroom apartment, located at 969 Park Avenue.

"Patsy and Johnny, pack up your toys and things. We are moving to a real classy neighborhood."

"But Mom, what about Nancy and my other friends?"

"You'll make new and better friends. The kids you will meet will have more class than the rowdy kids you now play with. And, Johnny give away that hockey stick. You certainly will not be playing in the street on Park Avenue!"

"Ah, Mom, must we?"

"Yes, and stop your sniveling."

I was absolutely devastated by this move away from 74th Street. Not only was I being separated from Nancy and my street friends but I now had to share a bedroom with my sister and Hiwa because there were only two bedrooms and my mother took one of them for herself. This was the first inkling that I had that my mother's love for my sister and I was the same love that she had for her possessions. When it came down to what was good for her and what was best for her children, she always won.

One of my mother's routines that I recall upset me, and I suppose my sister as well, was making us come into the living room from our bedroom when she had guests over for a party. She would introduce us as her precious jewels; however, before the party she would have admonished us with the expression that "children should be seen but not heard." I hated her friends for patting me on the head and saying what a handsome little man I was while totally ignoring my sister. After being sent back to our bedroom, Hiwa would let us come into her bed and comfort us because we were hurt by our mother's embarrassing behavior.

Another habit that she had that upset me even more was if her guests arrived after our bedtime, at around midnight, she would sneak her guests into our bedroom and turn on the lights to show off her precious possessions. Hilda, my sister, and I would pretend to be asleep, but the reality was that the noise that she and her guests made at the party kept us awake until well after they left for the evening. I swore that when I had children I would never do this to them, and I never did.

My sister and I went to Hunter Elementary School in New York City. Pat went on to high school at Hunter and was an honor student all the way through. I don't believe I was much of an achiever at Hunter. It really didn't matter as the school changed the rules and boys were not allowed to continue their education at Hunter after the sixth grade. My real education began the following year, 1942, when I was enrolled at Bordentown Military Institute.

THE BORDENTOWN MILITARY INSTITUTE YEARS
1942-1948

In April of 2002, I organized a mini-reunion for several of my fellow cadets from the graduation class of 1948. The reunion took place in Orlando, Florida. After fifty-four years, I did not know what to expect, and I had second thoughts and almost cancelled the affair. Luckily, I didn't. The two-day reunion was a rousing success and we had a great time swapping memories about our lives at B.M.I.

There were five of us, along with our wives, at this get together; Dick Kessler, Rick Memmoli, Eddie Bitter, Wes Finer and me. I had met with Dick and his wife Deb about six months earlier at the Atlantis Hotel in Reno, Nevada. I had not seen Dick in many years but found him through an Internet search where we were able to plan our visit in Reno. Dick always held a special place in my heart, as he was my roommate at Bordentown and one of my best friends. Dick went to Colgate University and after a stint in the military he became a very successful builder in NYC and other parts of the country. Dick is currently an investor and venture capitalist.

Rick and Eddie went to Duke University. Rick became a lawyer and is now retired and lives in Florida. Eddie, after serving in the navy went into his wife's family business, Scalamandre Silk. He and his wife, Adriana, are also retired and their children now run the business for them. Wes, who was my tennis partner at Bordentown, went to Yale University. He spent his entire career with the CIA and is also retired and lives in Florida.

At the opening cocktail party, Rick asked the rest of us if we would send our sons to B.M.I. Since the school does not exist anymore, it was really a theoretical question. The school closed during the Vietnam era when military schools lost favor with the public and could not survive without an adequate student population. I quickly answered Rick by stating emphatically that I would not send any son of mine to a school like Bordentown. However, I am going to answer Rick's question again after writing about the six years that I spent living and learning at B.M.I.

Chapter Two
Bordentown Military Institute

1942 - 1948

In September 1942, nine months after the United States entry into World War II, I arrived at Bordentown Military Institute. As a new cadet, I was required to arrive a week before classes were to begin. I attended various orientations, was assigned my dorm room, and was measured for, and received the uniforms that would be part of my life through grade and high school. I entered the 7th grade and would remain at Bordentown until I graduated from high school in 1948. The six years that I spent at B.M.I formed the foundation of my personality and established the core beliefs that I have adhered to for my entire life.

EDUCATION

One of the things I learned early on in my life is that perception sometimes appears more valid than reality. In the seventh and eighth grades I responded well to the discipline of being taught how to learn. At the end of each day, after we had our dinner, we were required to study and do our homework in the study hall, located in the school's main building. We were not permitted to talk. We were closely watched to ensure that we were studying and not playing games or reading novels. I had and still have a good short-term memory. Being forced to study enabled me to achieve high marks in my first subjects in the seventh and eighth grades. I soon got the reputation of being somewhat of a scholar and that served me well, as I managed to graduate as valedictorian of my class in 1948. The truth of the matter is that I got a lot of high marks because of my reputation for being smart. There were cadets that deserved better grades but did not have the same reputation.

The junior school at B.M.I. had sixty cadets beginning with the fourth grade through the eight grades. If I was amazed as to how anyone could send an eleven-year-old child to a boarding school, I am shocked at the thought of sending an eight-year-old off to a military academy. To ease the pain I suppose, we had a housemother, Caroline Ballis, whom we could turn to when we needed some mothering.

The subjects that I studied in the seventh and eighth grades were pretty standard: geography, history, language, arithmetic, and science. The only special course that was taught was Study Techniques. This subject, combined with small classes, and the enforced study hall, set me on the path to becoming an excellent student. At any rate, the seventh and eighth grades went by like a flash. In June of 1944, 21 of us graduated from junior school and went on to high school the following year. Of the 21 of us, ten, Nick Chergotis, John Elsasser, Charles Keach, Russ Laslocky, George Patrick, Paul Stanton, Jerry Wenig, Jay Woodward, Al Zlakowski, and I, went all the way through till graduation from B.M.I. in 1948.

In the 1944 *Sharpshooter*, which was the yearbook for the eighth grade graduating class, I had several achievements mentioned. I was the shortest -- unanimously. I was in a close tie for the thinnest with a cadet named Hunter. I was the best scholar, and I was in a tie with three other cadets for being the best storyteller.

One of the teachers about whom I have vivid and fond memories was Clarence Crobaugh. He taught classes in higher mathematics such as geometry, solid geometry, and trigonometry. He was a very stern taskmaster and when you were called to the front of the class to put a theorem on the blackboard (there were no vinyl boards in those days -- they were all black slate), you had better be right or you would stand there a long time till you got it correct. I remember one cadet who was so nervous when called on to go to the blackboard that he invariably wet his pants and had to be excused to go change his uniform. Luckily, I was very good in these subjects and earned top grades in all of them.

Brad Boone was a cadet with whom I was very friendly. He was a year ahead of me and graduated in 1947. In looking Brad up in the 1947 *Sword and Saber* (the class yearbook), I read the note he wrote to me: "Silby," (my nickname) "thanks for all the help you gave me in trigonometry." He added that he would not have passed without my help. I do not recall ever helping Brad out with his studies but I do remember lots of things about Brad Boone. His parents ran a nudist colony, "Sunshine Acres" located in Mays Landing, New Jersey.

On one spring break during my junior year at B.M.I, Brad invited Dick Kessler and me to a weekend at his parent's nudist colony. He assured us that we could go incognito, meaning that we could wear shorts and didn't have to be nude. It was a good thing that I remembered to take a tight jockstrap to wear under my shorts because I spent almost the entire weekend with an erection that wouldn't stop.

Dick and I arrived on a Friday evening in Dick's beautiful Mercury convertible that his parents had given him as a future graduation present. The first event that Brad had planned for us was a poker party since we all liked to play poker at Bordentown. Brad introduced us to his fiancée, Penny, to his sister, and to the other guests invited to the poker game. All of the players were stark naked except for Dick and me. We had our shorts on as well as sunglasses to prevent the others from seeing where our eyes were roaming. I don't know how Dick made out, but I lost my ass because concentrating on my cards was impossible.

The next day was spent playing volleyball, swimming, eating in the common dinning room, and generally goofing off. I was getting used to the scenery and actually had moments when the bulge in my shorts diminished. On Saturday evening, Brad invited Dick and me to meet him and Penny in Atlantic City to have dinner and see a show. When we met them in town and I did not recognize Penny, because this was the first time I had seen her with her clothes on and had more than a passing glance at her face. She was a very pretty girl and I believe that Brad married her that summer after he graduated from Bordentown.

One of the subjects that is not taught in school these days, but should be, is Latin. I had three years of Latin and won a medal for being best in my class at the end of the first year. Don't get me wrong; Latin itself has very little value as a spoken language, but was invaluable in teaching me the English language, especially grammar and sentence structure. It also served as a good foundation for learning other languages such as Spanish and French.

I loved taking drama classes and public speaking. This was probably the result of my having been active in these subjects while attending summer camp. My teacher was Ray Hurd who really encouraged me to compete in forensic speaking. I remember memorizing a speech from the movie *Tomorrow The World*. It started out; "My father was a traitor to the Third Reich." Unfortunately when I gave this speech, my voice was changing and cracked at inappropriate times. Instead of having the audience in a serious mood, I had them laughing. Needless to say, I did not win that contest. In the contest that I did win to become the south New Jersey Public Speaking champion, I gave the speech from Cyrano deBergerac in which he talks about his nose. Sadly, I lost in the New Jersey finals to a little Asian girl who beat me out in cuteness.

During my high school career at Bordentown, I was on the Honor Roll twelve times out of a possible twelve times and, as previously mentioned, was valedictorian of my graduating class in 1948. In retrospect, I believe that another cadet, Wes Finer, who wound up salutatorian probably should have been given the honor, but I had the reputation of being a scholar, whether deservedly or not. Many times in life I found that reputation carries more weight than achievement. For example, one time in my career, when I was working for Aerojet

General Corporation in Sacramento, California, I was asked to put a proposal together to develop a management information system for the local War-on-Poverty organization. I was asked to write the proposal because nobody else in the company would undertake the project. I was successful and that gained me the reputation as a proposal writer and management information specialist when in reality I was just lucky.

I think that the education that I received at Bordentown was excellent. Many of the teachers were first rate, the classes were small, and the subjects significant, plus they taught me how to learn. What they did not teach us was that in order to continue learning we had to maintain for ourselves the discipline that was forced on us at B.M.I. I enrolled at the Sibley School of Mechanical Engineering at Cornell University the fall following graduation. I lacked the discipline to force myself to study as much as engineering courses required, and at the end of my first semester I was put on probation.

MILITARY LIFE

The corps of approximately 250 cadets was divided into four companies and a band. "D" company was always the company for the junior school. In 1944, the year that I graduated from the eighth grade, the commanding officer of the company was George Patrick and I was the platoon sergeant. The military instruction for "D" company was learning how to march in formation and learning the manual of arms using the Springfield 03 rifle. Our military instructor was Sergeant Marshall who was assigned to B.M.I. by the army. Since this was wartime, the school expanded the military instruction covering such subjects as the Browning automatic rifle and the caliber 30 light machinegun.

Upon matriculating from junior school, we were assigned to one of the other three companies, or if we had any musical talent we were assigned to the band. We had to relinquish the ranks that we achieved in junior school and start all over as buck private freshman in high school. Over the next four years, I served in all three companies and in my senior year I was first sergeant of "A" company, commanded by Jay Woodward, who had graduated from grade school with me. After six years at Bordentown, I never achieved the rank of officer but did achieve the highest non-commissioned officer rank of first sergeant. I think there were quite a few reasons why I never made lieutenant, a rank that I coveted.

I was a small and skinny kid and did not project the image that the administration believed was necessary for commissioned officers. I found out later that this was truly a false criterion for becoming an officer. In 1953 I graduated from Officer Candidate School at Fort Benning, Georgia. After six grueling months, I weighed only 113 pounds, yet I was commissioned as an Infantry 2nd Lt.

Most of the cadets who achieved officer rank were the athletes or were tall good-looking kids. Another, probably more significant factor, was that I developed a rather wise-guy attitude and was especially critical of some of the school's administrators who I truly believed were anti-Semitic. I was especially critical of David Styer, the Chief Administrative Officer of Bordentown, who in my opinion was a real bigot. I think if it were not for my excellent academic record, Mr. Styer probably would have had me expelled for the insubordinate attitude that I developed. At any rate, I am sure that he prevented me from achieving what I wanted most at that time, which was to have all of the perks that came with being an officer.

Marching! Marching! Marching! We cadets marched everywhere. We marched to the study hall. We marched to the dining room. We marched in parades on holidays. We marched in competition against each other and we even marched to church.

Going to church on Sundays was an interesting experience for me as a Jewish cadet. There were no synagogues in Bordentown. Since there were a few Jewish kids at B.M.I., we were allowed to select which church we would march to on Sundays. Church was mandatory and once we decided which church we would attend we had to stay with that church for the entire year. My first year I decided to go to the Baptist church, and each year after that I selected a different denomination. In my senior year I went back to the Baptist church because they had the prettiest girls singing in the choir. After six years of sermons and false piety, I decided that I would never go to church again. I didn't, at least not until I was married in the Catholic Church as was requested by my beautiful Irish-Catholic bride.

Since there were no synagogues in the town of Bordentown, I had to take the train from Trenton to NYC to receive instruction in preparation for my Bar Mitzvah. Neither my father nor my mother really cared about this ceremony, but my grandparents insisted that I be a Bar Mitzvah when I reached my thirteenth birthday. My father engaged a rabbi, who for a little extra cash taught me the necessary Hebrew prayers phonetically. I never really learned Hebrew. On the big day I used all of my acting skills and performed so well that my grandparents never knew that I could not read or write Hebrew. I had committed the prayers to memory or read them phonetically in English. After this experience, not only did I decide that I would never attend church services again, I vowed that I would never set foot in a temple or synagogue for the rest of my life and I haven't, except for honoring others on special occasions.

Reveille during the week was at 7a.m. After we got dressed, made our beds, and cleaned our rooms, we would form by company in front of "Old Main" and march into the dining room for breakfast. "Old Main" was the building that housed the classrooms, the assembly hall, the dining room, and the gym.

The tables in the dining room would accommodate eighteen people. A teacher sat at the head of the table and if the teacher was married, his wife would sit on his left. The foot of the table was reserved for the highest-ranking officer or non-commissioned officer. Eight cadets would sit on each side of the table. We would remain standing until the cadet at the foot of the table would give the command to be seated. Next, the teacher in charge of the table would pick out a cadet to say grace. I still remember the grace that I said when I was called on to conduct this ceremony, "For this and all his mercies, God's holy name be praised." It was short and got us eating a lot sooner than some of the rambling prayers the other cadets put us through.

The best place to sit, I soon discovered, was somewhere in the middle of the table away from the eyes of the teacher or officer in charge. There was a game that we used to play called "Claim". The game consisted of sticking your fork into something on your neighbor's plate that you felt like eating. By the rules of the game, if you were successful in sticking your fork into a piece of meat or a potato, your neighbor had to forfeit the item and it became yours to eat. We all developed clever defensive strategies to ward off the attacking fork but sometimes the "Claim" attack was successful and we got a little extra to eat. There was an inherent risk in playing this game, however. If either the teacher or officer in charge caught us doing it, we would be dismissed from the table and go hungry until the next meal. We learned not to play the game until we had at least had something to eat.

After our morning classes were over we would assemble in the study hall where we had assigned seats and desks. After the "Orders of the Day" were read by the Officer of the Day, we would march, one row at a time, to the dining room. The "Orders of the Day" would specify what the uniform code would be for the following day, any promotions in rank that had occurred, what the athletic schedule would be, and any items of general interest to the entire cadet corps.

The food that they served us at Bordentown was first rate. The school employed a dietician who prepared the menus for each meal. I currently have two teenage grandsons and when the boys come for a visit, we never have enough in the house to fill them up. I can imagine what a daunting effort it must have been to feed 250 teenage cadets who were extremely active physically. One of the methods the school employed was that after we had finished our main course, more bread and potatoes would be placed on the table along with several boats filled with delicious meat gravy. It was rumored that the gravy was heavily laden with saltpeter which was a drug the administration believed would keep young libidos in check. We could have as much as we wanted, and after eating our fill, we were served dessert that would be ice cream with hot fudge sauce, or pie, or cake.

After dinner we had a half-hour break before having to return to our rooms or the study hall for the two-hour study period. I would use this break to go down to the "Hollow" which was the designated smoking area. We were required to have smoking permits in order to smoke but I never got a permit. My parents would never have allowed me to smoke. The school never enforced this policy so I started smoking at the tender age of eleven. Actually, I started smoking much earlier. When I was at Camp Kohut we would buy corncob pipes and smoke the silk that came off an ear of corn. The first few times I smoked corn silk, I threw up, but like anything else I got used to it and actually enjoyed it. Cigarettes were eleven cents a pack for such brands as Ramsey's or Wings. You could also buy individual cigarettes, called loosies, for a penny each. I smoked all my life, with a couple of failed attempts at quitting, until I turned sixty, and I have been-smoke free ever since.

SEX

I guess the saltpeter worked to a certain extent. You can imagine 250 adolescent males with raging hormones confined to a military institute without the normal means of exploration available to regular high school students. Well, certain events took place that made this aspect of our lives tolerable.

B.M.I. arranged dances three times a year with a girl's boarding school, Saint Mary's, located not too far from Bordentown. I'll never forget one evening prior to the first dance of the year. David Styer announced to the corps of cadets that we were indeed lucky that the school had arranged to secure the services of a famous band for our dance with Saint Mary's. He told us that this band had made famous one of the most popular songs of the times called "A dolly with a stocking in her hole." (What he meant to say was "A dolly with a hole in her stocking.") Two hundred and fifty cadets roared with laughter and were out of control for at least thirty minutes while that son-of-a-bitch tried to gain control. He turned red and I thought he was going to have a stroke which unfortunately did not happen

Before the dance, we did not know who our dance partners would be. It worked like this. The cadets would line up on one side of the gym where the dances were held, and the girls would line up on the other side. We would line up in order of height so that the tallest cadets would have as dance partners the tallest girls and so on. The teachers would introduce us to each other.

"This is Cadet Sergeant John Silberman"

"This is Mary Callahan."

"Pleased to make your acquaintance," the girl would say, and she would tuck her arm in mine and we would walk off across the gym while another couple was introduced to each other.

At one of the dances, one of my fellow cadets told me that Eddie Bitter's date had no hands. Eddie, one of my good friends and always the gentleman, never left that girl's side and danced with her the whole night through.

The dances with the girls from Saint Mary's were interesting affairs. We were instructed to have a minimum of two inches of space between our dance partners and our selves. This rule was enforced by the nuns of Saint Mary's and the teachers of B.M.I. who acted as chaperons during the dances. Since the girls of Saint Mary's boarding school were as horny as we were, as soon as a chaperon's back was turned, the two-inch rule went out the window. At one of the dances, my partner said to me with a suggestive smile, that I might be more comfortable if I took the pencil out of my pocket while we danced.

On weekends, if we did not have a pass to go home we would be permitted to go into town after the Saturday morning inspection took place. The inspection was very thorough. Our beds had to be made with military corners and if the inspector tossed a coin on the bed the covers had to be so tight that the coin would bounce. We had footlockers at the foot of our beds and everything in the footlocker had a precise destination. If the socks or gloves were in the wrong place you would fail inspection and lose the pass to town. They would inspect our rifles and if any rust or a speck of dust was found in the barrel, you failed inspection. The inspecting officer wore white gloves and would check our closets, doorsills, etc., and if he found any dust, that was another cause for failure. Needless to say, we spent a lot of time preparing for these inspections. We really wanted to get off campus for a few hours and would do whatever was required to obtain a pass.

Once in town we would have several choices of things to do. There was a movie theater, a bowling alley, and a pool parlor, but my favorite place was an ice cream parlor called "Mim & Bills." There was a long counter that ran down the front of the parlor and there were several booths that could seat about six people each. We would order ice cream sundaes, sodas, or banana splits and flirt with the town girls who came in groups of three or four.

One Saturday, in my freshman year, after having passed inspection, I was headed for "Mim & Bills". I walked past a bus stop and saw this cute little red-haired girl waiting for a bus.

" Hi. My name is Johnny. What's your name and where are you going?"

"My name is Glenna Bunick but my friends call me Bunny. I'm taking the bus to Trenton to visit with some of my cousins."

"Bunny, will you meet me next Saturday at 'Mim & Bills' for a soda?"

"Sure, Johnny, as long as I can bring one of my girlfriends too."

"No problem Bunny. I'll also bring one of my buddies with me. Have a nice trip to Trenton."

As luck would have it, the following Saturday, I brought my friend Nicholas Chergotis to the ice cream parlor to meet the girls. Bunny showed up with a beautiful Greek girl whose name I cannot recall but because of their ethnic background Nick and his date hit it off instantly.

Bunny was my girlfriend during my first and second year of high school. We would go to movies together, share sodas, go to dances, and even did a little necking when we had some privacy, which was not often. At a dance during my junior year, Bunny danced with one of my classmates, Paul Stanton, who was a tall good-looking kid who played on the varsity football team. Brains could not compete with brawn and Paul stole Bunny from me. He earned my enduring dislike for the rest of our time at Bordentown.

Many years later, while at Cornell University, I invited Bunny up to Ithaca for a weekend party at my fraternity, Alpha Epsilon Pi. We had a very nice weekend together but we both realized that we had grown apart and that weekend was the last time I ever saw her.

Back in the 1940's, there was a whole set of different moral standards. There was no such thing as HIV and AIDS. Promiscuity did not exist. Boys and girls dated each other, held hands, kissed, necked but, by and large, did not sleep with each other. Sexual intercourse was reserved for married couples or at the very least for couples that were engaged. There were very few couples who lived together without the benefit of marriage and those few that did were "shacking up." That does not mean that the cadets were pure of heart and did not think of sex with some degree of frequency. We use to regale each other with stories of our conquests that occurred during our vacations and summer recess. Most of the stories were pure fantasy, but we enjoyed them nonetheless.

I remember a story told to us before a history class by Dick Diener who graduated a year ahead of me in 1947. Dick lived in Baltimore, Md., and he told us that during the Thanksgiving vacation, his girlfriend had a very special present for him. The present was a pair of angora gloves that she put on before jerking Dick off. Well, about two weeks later at assembly hall, the Commandant of Cadets announced that during inspection they found angora gloves in our footlockers and since they were unauthorized, we had to get rid of them. It seems that despite the saltpeter, the heavy academic schedule, the athletics, and the military drills, the cadets were looking for new ways to masturbate.

SPORTS

Bordentown placed a lot of emphasis on sports. We had teams for football, soccer, basketball, baseball, track, tennis, and wrestling. Within each sport there was a varsity level, junior varsity level, junior level and midget level. Unfortunately, I was small and skinny; however, in my second year I played on the junior football team as a guard. but did not get much playing time. By the time I was a senior, I probably could have played football on the midget or junior teams, but I had too much pride to play on a team with kids much younger than I was.

The only sport that I excelled at was tennis. I played on the junior varsity team my first and second years and I was on the varsity squad during my junior and senior years. We played against other military or private schools like Admiral Farragut and Pennington. I was ranked seventh on the squad right behind Eddie Bitter and Wes Finer who were ranked fifth and sixth. I loved the competition and won more matches than I lost.

The football jocks were the most admired of all the cadets. There was a special L-shaped bench located right in front of the window where we could buy candy and other small items such as soap, toothpaste, etc. The football jocks appropriated this bench and they would swap stories about their exploits on the football field. During my senior year there was not too much to brag about because our varsity squad only won one game all season long. This was probably the worst team that Bordentown fielded during my six years. For some reason, the jocks kind of adopted me and would let me sit with them during their story telling sessions. I suspect it was because I would tutor some of them in subjects that they were having difficulty mastering. Although some of the jocks that I helped were just as smart as I was, they had to spend a lot of time practicing and their grades suffered as a result.

Coaches of the major sports such as football and basketball have a profound influence on the athletes that they coach. There was one SOB that sticks out in my mind. M.O. Borst (nicknamed Mob) coached both of these sports at both the varsity and junior varsity level. My friend, Dick Kessler, was a natural athlete and was also highly competitive. During his freshman year he played on the junior football team and on the junior varsity basketball team that was coached by Mob. As a sophomore, he played on the junior football team and on the varsity basketball team coached by Mob. As a junior he played JV football and JV baseball. During our senior year, Dick did not play for any of the teams as he had been totally turned off by what he perceived was the anti-Semitism displayed by coach Borst. This was not only too bad for Dick but too bad for the teams he could have played for, as his leadership and athleticism were unquestioned.

FRIENDS

When I look back at the six *Sword and Saber* (yearbooks) that I collected during my stint at Bordentown, tears come to my eyes as I recall the very many friends that I made over those formative years. A military boarding high school is unlike any other institution in the world. Young kids are thrown together in such an intense environment that the bonds that develop among the students are much stronger that what takes place in a conventional high school. As we were growing into young men, we would literally eat, play, learn, and sleep together in a highly charged atmosphere where dependence upon one another was essential for survival and sanity. An institution such as Bordentown is no substitute for a loving family and for those of us that did not come from a caring family, B.M.I. became the only family that we knew.

As I gaze at the pictures of my fellow cadets, both older and younger than I was, during those six years, so many memories come to mind that I probably could devote an entire book to the telling of these stories. In my senior year, I probably had at least a dozen of what I would consider to be my best friends, but I will limit the recording of my memories to two cadets, Dick Kessler and Dominick Acerra. Dom later became my first roommate at Cornell University. I truly believed that when I graduated in 1948 that I would remain fast friends with a number of my fellow cadets. The sad reality was that after college and a stint in the military, contacts with them were few and far between. After fifty years, through the magic of the Internet, I was able to make contact with a few of my special buddies and we had a great little reunion in April of 2002.

Dick Kessler arrived at Bordentown in the fall of 1944 as a freshman cadet. I had already been at Bordentown for two years attending the junior school. When I first met Dick as a fellow freshman,

I was wise to the ways of cadet life. I don't recall the circumstances of our first meeting but I know that I was thoroughly impressed with Dick. Not only was he an athlete, he was the most put-together individual that I had ever met. He was good-looking, intelligent, had a great sense of humor, could play the trumpet, and had a wonderful singing voice. Dick seemed to know what he wanted in life and was the most mature kid around. We use to call him "Mr. Mature" behind his back. Over the four years that we spent together, we became fast friends and I considered Dick one of my best friends at that point in my life. I believe that he felt the same way about me and as a matter of fact in our 1948 Year Book under the category of Senior Statistics Dick's "Favorite Place" was "with Silberman."

Dick really had a profound influence on my life. As seniors, we decided that we should attend the same college and be roommates again. We spent a weekend in Providence, Rhode Island and visited the Brown University campus. We both thought this would be a slick place to attend college since the all-girls college, Pembroke, was close by. As luck would have it, I was accepted to Brown but Dick wasn't. He was accepted at his second choice, Colgate University, and I was also accepted at my second choice, Cornell University. Dick made the decision to go to Colgate so I decided to go to my second choice, Cornell. I thought we would see each other frequently. Our class president Dominic Acerra was also going to Cornell and Dom and I decided to room together on campus.

During our senior year, Dick and I roomed together. We developed a fondness for the writing of Lin Yutan, a lapsed Catholic, who developed a rather unique philosophy. He believed that mankind was extremely egotistical to believe that God would give a hoot for an individual who is an infinitesimal speck on earth, which is an infinitesimal speck of the solar system, which is an infinitesimal speck of the universe. He believed that mankind should do good for the sake of doing good and not for the promise of some reward in heaven or the threat of bad things in hell.

I was the valedictorian of my class and had to deliver the valedictory speech as part of the commencement exercises. Dick helped me in the preparation of my speech that quoted heavily from Lin Yutan's philosophy. Dean Smith was the academic dean of the school and he had to approve my speech before I could deliver it. Dean Smith, being a devoutly religious man, would not even consider any part of my writings and sent me back to do a complete re-write. I was instructed that this heretical philosophy was not appropriate material for a commencement address.

I went back to the drawing board, and prepared another, totally innocuous, document that met with the approval of Dean Smith and the other teachers in charge of the graduation ceremonies. When commencement day finally arrived, I memorized both speeches — the one that I presented to Dean Smith and the original one that I actually delivered as my valedictory statement. Dick and a few of my other buddies were in on the plan and the thunderous applause that I received upon completion of my speech even brought a smile to Dean Smith's face; I rather expected that he would have had me shot off the podium.

Around the spring of our junior year Dick and I became rather disillusioned about life at B.M.I. Dick's disillusionment was probably the result of the unfair treatment that he received from coach Borst. Mine came from having been at Bordentown for over five years with the realization that I would never be promoted to be an officer. One Saturday afternoon we had somehow managed to purchase a pint of Philadelphia whiskey. We sat on a log on the "hill" and drank the whole pint with the expected result of becoming totally smashed. This was only the second time in my life and certainly not the last time that I was thoroughly drunk.

The preceding New Years eve, Rick Memmoli had invited a bunch of his classmates over to his house for a party. The only alcoholic beverage that I had tasted before this party was beer. Rick had a variety of alcoholic beverages available to us in addition to beer. I decided on Southern Comfort which had a surprisingly sweet taste to it. After a few hours and several Southern Comforts, I became quite dizzy and raced upstairs to the bathroom. On the way to the toilet to throw-up I managed to crack my head open on the bathroom sink.

"Not to worry", said Rick, whose family consisted of four generations of doctors. He poured a bottle of peroxide on my scalp and covered the entire top of my head with a huge bandage that he taped under my chin and then put me to bed.

The next morning Rick drove me to my stepmother Ida's house located in McDougal Alley in Greenwich Village. I was afraid of the tirade that would occur if I went back home to my mother. Ida cleaned me up and sobered me up and I was able to go home without my mother ever knowing what happened. To this day I cannot look at a bottle of Southern Comfort without getting queasy and now that I am bald I have the scar to prove the stupidity of youth.

On numerous Christmas or spring vacations, Dick would invite me to his home for a weekend visit and we would share a room in the top floor of his parent's home in Flushing, New York. His mom and dad were wonderful people and treated me like I was Dick's brother. Sidney, Dick's father, was a prominent builder of houses and apartment buildings in Long Island and New York City. I believe the Kesslers were very wealthy. You would never know it from the way they conducted themselves. Dick had a younger sister, Betty, who tagged along with us when we went to Dick's parent's country club at Atlantic Beach. Since we were interested in trying to pick up girls at the club we always found a way to ditch poor Betty. I understand that Betty became, and probably still is, a prominent judge in Florida.

The one thing I could not do was reciprocate and invite Dick to my mother's apartment on Park Avenue. I had learned a long time before never to invite any of my friends to visit at my home. My mother would embarrass me terribly by the questions she would ask them and the name-dropping that was part of her style. I never once had anyone visit me at my mother's apartment until I became engaged to Barbara. I gave Barbara a thorough briefing as to what to expect and bless her Irish heart, my mother could not get to her until quite a few years had passed.

On weekends during our senior year a bunch of us cadets, Bernie Levy, Dick, Rick Memmoli, and Eddie Bitter and I would go down to Greenwich village to hear some jazz and visit the strip joints. There was one club in particular that we favored called "Pinto's." There was a comedian that we especially liked who had a funny, dirty version of the song "Chicago." There was also a good-looking blonde stripper that would sit with us after her performance and we would buy her drinks and swap stories with her.

One Saturday night Dick and I were in "Pinto's" without the other fellows. This stripper was probably about 27 or 28 whereas Dick and I were about 17 or 18. At closing time, my buddy Dick, "Mr. Mature" asked this chick if she would like to come home with us. To my surprise and delight, she agreed. My mother was out of town so this was the first opportunity that I had to invite Dick to the apartment on Park Avenue. We got to the apartment and Dick and our new friend went immediately into my mother's bedroom presumably not to swap stories. I thought that I might have my way with her after Dick, but it was not to be. I know Dick is a truly generous person and we had shared many things in life but not this girl. I believe she liked Dick so much that she thought she could establish a serious relationship with him. We shared a watered-down drink after they were finished with my mother's bedroom. They left my apartment and I went to bed that night thinking what might have been if I were "Mr. Mature."

As our final year was winding down I was getting more and more disillusioned with life at Bordentown. I was so anxious to get on with the rest of my life that Dick and I even decided to skip the senior prom. We always had great bands at our proms because of the connection we had with Eddie Davis of "Leon & Eddie's" nightclub. As a matter of fact, in my sophomore year, we had Louie Prima's band featuring Keely Smith, the beautiful singer. That was the dance that I took Bunny to, where Paul Stanton stole her from me.

On Commencement day, after all the speeches were completed, there was one last march that took place. During the march, First Lieutenant Richard Memmoli, Second Lieutenant Richard Kessler, and First Sergeant John Silberman separated ourselves from our respective companies, joined together, and slowly marched off the parade field in what was, I suppose, a last act of defiance towards Bordentown Military Institute.

The following year Dick and I went off to our respective colleges and time and distance impacted our friendship.

At our reunion in Florida during April 2002, Rick Memmoli asked the question as to whether I, in retrospect, would send my son to B.M.I. I answered no, and that would still be my answer. I think a better question would be that if I had a choice, would I have gone to Bordentown? The answer to that question, Rick, is an unequivocal yes. I believe that my father probably enhanced my life by sending me away from my mother.

More importantly, I learned, at Bordentown, the values and core beliefs that I have followed for my entire life. We were taught, "Good, Better, Best, Never, Never Rest Till Your Good Is Better And Your Better, Best." I have always strived to be the best in whatever I was doing. We were taught, "Rather Be, Than Seem." I have never pretended to be anything but what I am. All the people in my life can testify to the fact that what you see in Silberman is what you get. We were taught discipline, loyalty, and how to learn, all of which served me well over the years.

Chapter Three
Cornell University

1948 - 1952

Before heading off to college, I had a lot of shopping to do. For the previous six years my wardrobe consisted of military uniforms with just a few civilian clothes thrown into the mix. My father gave me a few hundred dollars to buy college clothing and because he hated to shop, I asked my sister to help me pick out a wardrobe for my new life as a college student.

We selected four double-breasted suits with the appropriate ties, shirts, socks, and sweaters. Pat also helped me pack for the train trip to Ithaca where Cornell was located. I originally thought I would drive to Cornell because I had expected a car as my graduation present from Bordentown. Instead I was given an English ten-speed bicycle. I was sorely disappointed because my dad had a new Ford convertible with wooden sides that he hinted would be mine. I hated that damn bike and never rode it and have no idea what became of it.

Pat did a great job of packing. She placed the trousers, shirts, and ties in one suitcase, and the jackets and sweaters in the other suitcase. The trip from Penn Station to Ithaca, New York, took about ten hours so I had a sleeping compartment. I had placed my two suitcases and my typewriter outside my sleeping compartment and when I woke up the next morning I discovered one of my suitcases was missing. When I got to my dorm, I unpacked the one suitcase that I had left only to discover that I had four double-breasted jackets, some sweaters, and no trousers, shirts, or ties. This required emergency shopping because my roommate, Dom Acerra, was twice my size and could not lend me any of his clothing. I learned a valuable lesson and nobody has ever packed for me again.

The trip up to Ithaca was quite an experience. Aside from having one of my suitcases stolen, I observed what I thought was rather bizarre behavior. I had just graduated from a strict military school environment. I was not used to seeing a bunch of college age kids drinking vast quantities of beer and booze. Not being a person to be left out of things, I joined the party on the train and became snookered for the third time in my life. I woke up the next morning with a fierce hangover. I was not in the best of moods after discovering my suitcase missing but things went from bad to worse. I was standing on the platform with my one remaining suitcase and my typewriter and hailed a cab to take me to my dorm. Just as I was about to enter the cab, the door on the other side of the cab was jerked open and a voice said to me, "Sorry, pal, this is my cab now." And the cab sped off.

I found out later that the student who stole my cab was Bob Davidson, who eventually became my roommate, and was, and still is, one of my best friends. Bob is retired now; he remarried and moved to Guadalajara, Mexico to live. The marriage did not work out so Bob left Mexico and moved to Carson City and has an apartment close to where Bobbie and I live.

As an engineering student, I was enrolled in the Sibley School of Mechanical Engineering at Cornell University. I really had no desire to become an engineer, but since my dad had many patents on zipper making machines, he kind of pushed me in that direction. It's interesting in that while he never graduated from high school, he was a practical engineering genius. It did not take long for me to discover that I had made the wrong choice in professions.

One of my first subjects as a freshman was mechanical drawing. I purchased a drafting set which consisted of a compass and several other specialized tools used for mechanical drawing. The set also had a specialized eraser, which was the tool that got the most use from me. There are two skills that are necessary to become a successful draftsman; a steady hand, and the ability to visualize objects in three dimensions. I possessed neither of these abilities, and as a matter of fact, my shaky hands got me into future trouble both in law school and in the business world. Try as I might, I could not master this subject and I received a "D" grade in it at the end of the first semester. I probably deserved an "F" grade but the instructor took pity on me for trying to get it right with the heavy use of my eraser.

Another subject that I had difficulty with was Physics. The subject was taught in a large amphitheater that seated over two hundred students. During the first class, the professor stood in the middle of the classroom and held what looked like a miniature bowling ball to his head. The ball was tethered to a chain that was suspended from the middle of the ceiling. The professor released the ball and it slowly traveled to the other end of the classroom. It then started to swing back to where the professor was still standing. I don't have a clue as to what principle he was trying to teach. All I knew was that the ball was going to smash into his head and I would have one dead professor during my first class in Physics. Luckily the ball stopped a few inches from his nose. To this day, I don't know what he was trying to teach, but that was one of the weirdest demonstrations I have ever witnessed.

There were many contributing factors in my journey from graduating as valedictorian of my high school class to being placed on probation at the end of my first semester in college. One of the most significant factors was the presence of girls in my classes. Coming from an all-male military institute to a coed college was quite an experience. To say they were a distraction would be putting it mildly. It seemed that they all wore angora sweaters that reminded me of Dick Diener's story. I had been taught how to take notes while the teacher was lecturing, which I did. The majority of the girls would be knitting while the lecture was going on, and never took any notes. When it came test time, they invariably had higher scores than I did, perhaps because my notes were not so accurate because of all those sweaters I was admiring.

Another big factor in my failing the first semester was my

roommate, Dom Acerra, a very likable fellow who was elected class president during my senior year at Bordentown. Dom was a big, good-looking, athletic guy, enrolled as a pre-med student at Cornell. The courses that pre-med students took their first couple of years were pretty easy compared to what was required of engineering students. After a tough day of classes and faced with many hours of homework, I would come back to the dorm and find Dom getting dressed up to go to one of the many freshmen dances that took place at Cornell. After a few nights of being a good boy and buckling down to do my homework, I finally said, "To hell with it" and asked Dom to wait for me while I gussied myself up for the dance. For an engineering student, it does not take long to fall behind if you don't keep up with your homework, and that is exactly what happened to me.

Dom and I had a great time as roommates during our first semester in college. Entering freshmen get "rushed" by a number of fraternities early in the school year. Back in those days fraternities and sororities were pretty much segregated based on your religious background. Since a lot of Jewish kids went to Cornell, I had eleven Jewish fraternities that "rushed" me. There was only one Catholic fraternity; so poor Dom did not have much of a choice. However, I fixed that problem. When the brothers would come to pick me up for a visit at their frat houses, I would introduce my roommate, as Dom Acerraberg, and he would automatically be invited to accompany me on the visit. Those visits were really parties designed to see if your personality was a good fit with the group. I eventually joined Alpha Epsilon Pi and Dom joined the Catholic fraternity.

After Dom and I joined our respective fraternities, we spent spend less time together because our social lives now centered within the fraternities. An unfortunate event occurred towards the end of the first semester, which resulted in Dom's expulsion from Cornell University. I wasn't present, but I understand that during a chemistry lab, Dom and the chemistry instructor got into an argument and Dom belted the instructor and knocked him out. Dom transferred to the University of Alabama and subsequently became a doctor. I never saw Dom again but I did try to contact him many years later. I called information in Red Bank, New Jersey, Dom's hometown, and found the number for a Doctor Acerra. I called and left a message with his office but I never received a return call. A few months ago, I received a B.M.I. alumni newsletter that contained the information that Dom had passed away.

After Dom left Cornell, I decided to move out of the dorm and move into the A.E.P. fraternity house. That's when I became reacquainted with Bob Davidson, the student who stole the taxi from me on my first college day. Bob and I were on opposite sides of an election for our fraternity pledge president. I supported a pledge by the name of Morty Cooper mainly because Morty had a car and I knew if I could get him elected I would have access to some transportation. Bob supported Al Kresh, a likeable fellow who, however, did not have wheels. Through superior debating skills I was able to muster enough votes to have Morty elected pledge president and Bob's candidate, Al, was defeated. After this debate, Bob and I got to know each other, and became friends throughout college, and indeed friends for life, although I am still pissed off at him for stealing that cab.

As anticipated, at the end of my first semester, I was placed on probation. I received failing grades in Calculus, Chemistry, and Mechanical Drawing. The only subjects that I did well in were liberal arts courses such as English and American History. I had to make a decision. If I decided to stick with Engineering, I would have to repeat the subjects that I failed. I knew in my heart that no matter how hard I tried, I would never master Mechanical Drawing so I decided to transfer to another major. My friend, Bob Davidson, was enrolled in the New York State School of Industrial and Labor Relations at Cornell so I made the decision to transfer to his major.

This was an excellent choice. For engineering students, two plus two has to equal four. For an I.L.R. student, two plus two could be twenty-two or four or anything in between depending on which arguments would be put forth. Precision was never my thing. In Labor Relations, you could take many different positions on any subject, since there really was no one right answer. I flourished in this environment and never failed another subject, with one exception.

In our junior year Bob and I were living with two other fellows, Toby Silverman and Joe Corso, in an apartment in downtown Ithaca. Naturally, we would have to cook our own meals and since neither Bob nor I were very proficient in that department, we decided to enroll in a cooking course that was given by the Home Economics Department. We had to get special permission to sign up for this course because it was reserved for Cornell coeds only. The fact that it was a girl's only class was probably the real reason that we took that course.

It was like being back in engineering school all over again except the students were a heck of a lot prettier. The recipes and the cooking times were very precise and the teacher did not tolerate any experimentation, which I was prone to do. I got a "D" in soufflé making (I could never get the damn thing to rise). In addition to learning how to cook, the course was also intended to teach us how to set the table and how to serve the meal properly. My job during the final exam was to serve the meal, consisting of fried chicken and corn on the cob to the students at my table. I didn't realize that the teacher was standing directly behind me, as I was about to serve the chicken and the corn. One of the girls at the table motioned for me to use my hands to serve these items rather than the appropriate utensils, which I did. There was much giggling, with the exception of the teacher who did not think my serving style was funny at all. At any rate, that did me in and the teacher gave me a failing grade which I truly deserved. To this date, I am not very good in the kitchen although I can do a hell of a barbeque outdoors.

As a freshman, I tried out for the tennis team. Unfortunately, the level of talent on the Cornell tennis team far exceeded my skills. I did not even come close to even making the junior varsity squad. I really felt the need to participate in some type of sporting activity. When one of my fraternity brothers, Paul "Canvasback" Cohen invited me to join the boxing club, I accepted. Because I had some boxing instruction from my father's buddy, Lou Staff, I felt that could probably do well as a college boxer. Professor Marchant, who was also the

American History teacher, coached the fighters in the club.

I boxed as a flyweight, which was for men who weighed 120 pounds or less. Since I was relatively tall for someone who weighed so little, I enjoyed quite a bit of success. This was because I had a reach advantage over most of my opponents. In 1950, I fought for the championship of that weight class. The kid I was going to fight was a well-conditioned athlete and was the coxswain of the varsity crew.

My fraternity brothers and I devised a psychological strategy designed to fake this kid out. When he was at the club, I would get in the ring and spar with one of my fraternity brothers, Noel Mermey, who weighed about 175 pounds. We would spar for a few minutes and then I would punch Noel in the head and he would fall over pretending that I had knocked him out. I did this with Noel and several other of my bigger fraternity brothers and I knew I had this kid's attention.

The night of the big fight arrived. There were about 500 students and teachers in attendance at Barton Hall, the location for the championship fights. My second, Noel Mermey, and two of my girlfriends, Florence Falk and Elaine Rose, escorted me down the aisle, to the sound of thunderous applause. Mine was the first fight of the evening as we fought in order of our weight classification. When we were introduced to the crowd, I could see that my opponent's knees were trembling because he was about to fight a giant killer.

This was a three-round fight and the first round belonged to me because my opponent kept backing away from my jabs as if I was going to hurt him. Towards the end of the second round, he started to get wise to me. I was hitting him with all that I had and he realized that I could not put him down. The third round was his; he started to beat the daylights out of me and I had all I could do to keep my feet under me. Since I had won two out of the three rounds, I won the fight and received a gold medal as champion of the flyweight division. After that fight, I wisely retired from boxing and never ever boxed again. Quitting when you are ahead still sounds good to me. Well, maybe.

One night about six months ago, Bobbie and I were sitting at the Sports Bar in the Carson Station having a glass of wine and playing the video poker machine, which is what we do after having dinner. Bobbie was sitting on my left and on my right was a young fellow who was explaining to Doug, the bartender, that although he was working at "Big O" as a tire changer, he was really an inventor who was going to be quite rich some day. Doug paid him the appropriate attention so he started to talk to several of the cocktail waitresses who were collecting drinks at their workstation to his right. He started to pick on one waitress who was visibly pregnant. He told her that she probably did not know who the father was since she obviously was the kind that slept around a lot. When I saw her becoming flustered and teary-eyed, I told this guy to mind his manners if he knew what was good for him. I guess the security guards heard what was going on, because when the jerk told me "to shut the fuck up," I belted him and knocked him off his bar stool. Security surrounded us in seconds and since Barbara and I are well known in all the bars and gin mills in Carson City, they escorted this fellow out and told him never to return. We left the Station and did not return for a few days. When I finally got the nerve to go back to the Sports Bar I was greeted with applause, and a "Here's Rocky!" The cocktail girls and bartenders all called me "Rocky" all evening. Not bad for a seventy-year-old guy.

During our second year, Bob Davidson and I lived in the Alpha Epsilon Pi fraternity house. We were not roommates yet, but we were starting to develop a strong friendship. Living in a fraternity was quite a trip. Our fraternity was not like "Animal House" because the focus was on academic achievement; however, there was no shortage of parties and dances to attend. The ratio of male students to coeds was about four to one, so in order to get a date with a Cornell coed required quite a bit of planning. The girls would book a date with you for several weeks in advance. I started to date Florence Falk, who was in several of the classes that Bob and I took in the I.L.R. School. I was also dating a girl by the name of Elaine Rose who was in my history class. I would take one or the other to the dances at the fraternity house. After a couple of months I knew that something was fishy because I would tell one of the girls something and the other one would know about it. I discovered that Florence and Elaine were roommates and were just playing with me. After that discovery, the three of us would go out together and if that meant going to a movie, Bob would occasionally join us.

Three times a year at Cornell there was a big weekend party. The guys would give up their rooms at the fraternity and turn them over to the girls who were invited for the weekend. Since the Cornell coeds gave us a hard time by making us wait weeks in advance before allowing us a date, it was universally understood that for these special parties only "imports" were invited. It was to one of these parties that I invited Bunny, my Bordentown girlfriend from years ago, only to discover that we had very little in common anymore. At another party, I invited Noel Troy who was a beautiful model and the daughter of one of my mother's best friends. What a disaster that weekend was!

Alpha Epsilon Pi was a Jewish fraternity and by charter, only Jews were allowed to join. We decided to challenge the fraternity's charter by accepting a Christian kid, Ronny Farish, who was a close friend of one of the brothers. Well, I knew something was rotten in Denmark when I went down to the train station to pick up my date, Noel. I had met Noel only once when she and her mother were visiting my mother in New York. We had gone out to a movie and that was the only date I had with her before inviting her to the Cornell weekend party. She was extremely cold to me when I picked her up at the station and barely talked to me on the way to the frat house. To this day, I don't know what the problem was but as soon as she met Ronny, I was dust and she spent all of her time with him and totally ignored me. I spent the entire weekend getting blitzed, and if she got back to the train station for her trip back to New York, Ronny must have taken her because I certainly didn't.

During my second year at Cornell, I became pretty active in my fraternity's affairs and was elected social chairman. This was a great job because not only did I plan the parties and dances, I was responsible for ordering the booze. Some of the students formed their own bands and I came across a great one by the name of "Icky, Abby, and Foo". These guys were great musicians and, as musicians were wont to do in those days, smoked marijuana, ("Mary Janes" back then). I had them play at several of our functions and they would invariably offer me a joint. Because I smoked cigarettes and drank plenty of Scotch, I decided that this was one more vice that I did not need. Because I got to order the booze, the liquor salesman would include an especially good bottle of Scotch that Bob and I would appropriate for our own personal consumption.

Towards the end of our second year, Bob and I were getting a little tired of life in a fraternity house and we decided to rent an apartment for our junior year in downtown Ithaca. My father had bought me a car, a 1950 Nash Rambler convertible, and since Bob and I mostly took the same classes together, getting to the campus from downtown was no problem. I got the car in the summer between my first and second years at Cornell. My dad was in one of his flush periods and bought both my sister and me twin Nash Ramblers; hers was green and mine was tan. He also bought himself a black convertible Hudson that was driven by his new friend and chauffeur, Larry Gabbelli. I was not a very experienced driver so I asked my friend Rick Memmoli to meet me at my dad's office and help me drive the car home. It was raining cats and dogs that day and Rick helped me get the car home and then he took a subway ride back to his house.

In our junior year, we found and rented a two-bedroom apartment in a building owned by a local podiatrist. Bob and I shared one bedroom and Toby Silverman occupied the second bedroom. Toby was one of our fraternity brothers. He was a World War II veteran and was enrolled in the School of Agriculture. After a couple of months it became apparent that the three of us were having difficulty coming up with the rent so we decided to look for a fourth roommate.

We placed an ad in both the local and student newspaper. The ad specified, "If you wear white-buck shoes you needn't apply". It seemed like most of the Cornell undergraduates wore white-buck shoes and talked like Jimmy Stewart, who spoke as if he had a mouthful of marbles. The three of us did not want a roommate like that and what we got instead was Joe Corso, a World War II vet, and an engineering student. Joe was a very conscientious and we did not see all that much of him. Both he and Toby were serious about their studies and they both spent a lot of time attending classes or studying in the library. Not Bob and I. Either the courses that they taught us in the school of Industrial and Labor Relations were easy, or we took to them naturally. Neither Bob nor I spent a lot of time studying, and as a matter of fact, we cut a lot of classes but still maintained decent averages in all of our subjects.

We developed a passion for movies and occasionally would see two double features in the same day. I know there was a stretch of twenty-two straight days when we saw a movie every day. Maybe that's why I haven't gone to a movie theatre in over twenty years and only occasionally rent them from the video store. Another passion we developed was playing poker. Bob was an excellent poker player and he would use his winnings to supplement the rather meager allowance that he got from his parents. I recall several times when we would play poker all night and then have to attend a class in the morning. Sometimes there were classes that we just couldn't cut. We would swallow a couple of "No-Doz" tablets and tough it out.

Towards the end of my junior year, I applied for, and was accepted as an intern for the New York State Board of Mediation. This was a summer job located in Syracuse, New York. I knew that I would be assisting a state mediator in resolving real labor disputes. In order to look older and more mature, I decided to grow a mustache. I made the mistake of telling my sister about my plans and on their next visit to Cornell, my sister, my father, and Ida all got off the plane wearing fake mustaches. Naturally, this was designed to encourage me to shave mine off, but it had the opposite effect, and I let it grow bushier.

Irv Shapiro was the New York State mediator that I was assigned to for the summer. Irv was an attorney and was one of the hardest working individuals that I have ever met. He took me under his wing and taught me when it was appropriate to have both labor and management in one room and when it was necessary to separate them during the mediation process. One of the techniques that he employed was wearing the parties out so they would come to some sort of an agreement. Irv had fantastic stamina and he would keep the negotiation going for twenty-four hours or longer until both sides were so tired they would agree to anything just to put an end to the talks.

Once Irv developed some confidence in me, he would place me in charge of either the labor group or the management group when it was time to conduct the mediation separately. At first, I was pretty nervous but I learned how to narrow the issues so that when it was time to bring both sides back together, Irv would have a better shot at reaching a settlement. Irv and I spent many hours together during that summer and became close friends. After about a month of working with Irv he invited me to stay at his home in Cazenovia so I gave up my apartment in Syracuse and moved in with him, his lovely wife and young son, Seth. This internship was one of the best jobs that I ever had and I learned a lot that has been useful for my entire life. I visited with Irv a few times after that summer but our lives went in different directions and we lost touch with each other.

My senior year at Cornell was rather uneventful except for forming a relationship with Cathy Webster, a student at Wells College in Aurora, New York. Wells College was an all-girls' school located about forty-five minutes from Cornell. It was a lot easier getting a date at Wells than it was dating a Cornell coed so a bunch of my friends and I would travel in my car for a weekend visit with the girls of Wells college. It so happened that my childhood friend, Nancy Weil was a student there. I tried to date Nancy but she was engaged at that time to a fellow from Yale University, She did, however, introduce me to Cathy and we started going together.

Cathy lived in New York City not too far from my mother's apartment. One weekend during a holiday break, I picked up Cathy at her parents home in Manhattan. Her father, a lawyer in the prestigious firm of Sullivan and Cromwell, cross-examined me about my background and religious beliefs. It was apparent to me that Mr.

Webster did not approve of me as a suitable suitor for his daughter. We went out to dinner and a movie that evening, but I must say that her father's attitude put a damper on our relationship.

We continued to date for a while when we returned to college, but it was not long before I received the expected "Dear John" letter. On the Saturday following the receipt of Cathy's letter, I started to drink quite heavily. Bob made some disparaging remark about Cathy so I grabbed the bayonet that his brother had captured from a German soldier during World War II and started to chase him around the apartment. Thank God he was too fast for me and all I succeeded in was carving up some of our furniture. After I got the hostility out of my system, I decided it would be a good idea to drive to Wells College and see if it might be possible to patch up my friendship with Cathy. It was snowing like crazy and I was as drunk as a skunk and had no right to be driving anywhere. About halfway to Aurora, I went off the road, hit a rock, and flipped the car over. In any other convertible I would have been dead. The design of the Nash Rambler convertible is what saved my life. Both the driver and passenger sides had steel rails over the windows that the canvas top rode back on. The rails did not buckle which prevented my head from hitting the ground. A couple of farmers came by and pulled me out of the car. I did not have a scratch or bruise anywhere. They say that God protects fools and drunks and He certainly protected this foolish drunk. If I had behaved like that in this day and age, I would have gotten a DUI and probably would have done some jail time. Back in the 1950's the rules for drinking and driving were much different and the public was not as concerned about it as they are today.

Needless to say, I did not see Cathy that day and as a matter of fact, I never ever saw her again. I had the car towed back to Ithaca where it was totaled and went off to the junkyard. My dad was a real sport about this mishap and when I went back to New York over the Christmas holiday he gave me his new Hudson convertible to finish out my final year in college. The car was gorgeous. It was black with a red leather interior that made dating a snap.

Because of my positive experience with Irv Shapiro and my

mother's constant nagging that I had to have a profession, I decided to apply for admission to law school. I took the LSAT and scored quite high. I applied and was accepted at Harvard, Yale, and Columbia Law Schools. I did not want to make a decision as to which school I would go to until the summer after graduating from Cornell. The police action in Korea was going strong and I was not sure if I wanted to go into the service or attend law school with a student deferment. As valedictorian of my class at B.M.I. I had automatically received an appointment to West Point. I declined this appointment as I had had six years of military school and was sick of it and wanted to go to a college near my friend, Dick Kessler. Because of going to Bordentown, I could also have attended the senior R.O.T.C. program at Cornell and would have been commissioned as a 2nd Lt. upon graduation. I declined this as well.

Bob and I had become really bored with college life and could not wait to graduate and leave Ithaca forever. The day finally came when we received our B.S. degrees but neither of us took the trouble to attend the graduation ceremonies. We just packed up and headed home. I never kept up with the Cornell Alumni Association, and to this day I am listed as "Among the Missing."

Chapter Four
Military Service

1952 - 1955

When I graduated from college, I moved back to New York City fully expecting to have my own apartment. That was not to be. My father was in one of his periodic down periods and could not afford to give me the money to rent an apartment in Manhattan, and my mother wouldn't. I moved back in with her and had to listen to her constant criticism of my smoking, drinking, and choice of friends.

The only way out was to get a job and accumulate enough money to be able to rent and furnish an apartment by myself. I would not have minded sharing a place with one of my friends but I did not even have enough money for that. So, I started to network with my buddies, and Rick Memmoli discovered that the Schaefer Brewing Company was hiring recent college graduates to become sales representatives. Schaefer hired Rick, Bob Davidson, and me knowing full well that it would not be a full-time commitment because we all were either going into the service or would be going on to graduate school.

What a great job! I don't know why Schaefer required a college degree because the courses that I took in college had nothing to do with the sale of Schaefer beer "with the full flavor that's light and dry too." Schaefer Brewery was located on Kent Avenue in Brooklyn. I had to drive from Manhattan to Brooklyn to pick up my route for the day and then drive to the Bronx where my territory was located. This made absolutely no sense to me. I wanted a territory in Manhattan where I lived. The powers that be did not want to change my route, and because I needed the job, I just had to put up with the extra driving.

As a Schaefer salesman, my route consisted of mainly grocery stores and delicatessens with a few bars a day thrown into the mix. There was a special advertising campaign going on that summer with the slogan, "Schaefer rings the bell with the full flavored beer that's light and dry too." I was given a little bell and was told that when I went into a bar to sell the bartender some canned or bottled Schaefer beer, I was to ring the bell and repeat the slogan. Next, I was to ask the patrons at the bar if I could buy them a glass of Schaefer beer.

Well, the first bar that I went in, I did as I had been told, and the big beefy bartender said that if I didn't stop "ringing that stupid bell he would shove it up my ass." The barflies that were sitting around at 9a.m. that morning got a good laugh out of my embarrassment, and the bartender told me if I was going to buy his patrons anything it better be a shot of what they were already drinking. I threw that bell in the garbage and at the next bar on my route, I asked the bartender if I could buy the guys at the bar a shot of their favorite booze with a Schaefer beer chaser. That seemed to work and I got a nice order for several cases of Schaefer beer. Live and learn.

My summer as a beer salesman went along beautifully; however, I had to make a decision as to which law school I would attend. I did not achieve my goal of saving enough money to have my own apartment but I had enough to pay for my first semester of law school if I continued to live with my mother. So the choice was really made for me; I could not afford to live at an out-of-town law school; therefore, it had to be Columbia.

I started Columbia Law School in September of 1952 but I never really got with the program. I was miserable living at home and all my buddies were going into the service for the Korean War (police action). The Korean War was pretty horrible, but unlike Vietnam, there were no war protestors, and when it came time to serve your country, you served. The attitude back then was that if your government said some foreign forces threatened it, you did not question it. When you registered for the draft and were indeed drafted, you did not go to Canada, you went into the military. Of course, there were exceptions to this, and because I was enrolled in law school, I had a student deferment.

I am not a jingoistic patriot but I felt uneasy having a deferment when all of my friends were going into the various services, one by one. I made the decision to quit Columbia Law School and enrolled in the army on October 21, 1952. Because I had not gone to R.O.T.C. at Cornell, I found myself as a buck private at Camp Kilmer in New Jersey. After being issued my uniform and given the mandatory skinhead haircut, I was assigned to my barrack, and lo and behold, who was in the bunk two down from mine, none other than Bob Davidson. He was in bed suffering from something that he called monkey fever. Bob explained to me that he probably got this sickness as a result of an experiment the army was conducting concerning the breakfast meal. I didn't believe what he told me, but when I had my first army breakfast of peanuts and orange juice, I believed him.

My first assignment in the army was also unbelievable. While waiting to be assigned to a basic training company, I was given a pair of scissors and told to cut the grass in front of the major's quarters. When I questioned the sanity of the sergeant who gave me that stupid assignment, I was ordered to do twenty pushups and then preceded to cut the grass with my trusty scissors. Luckily, I was assigned to a basic training company after just a few days of gardener duty. I would now learn how to be a soldier in the U.S. Army.

The eight weeks of basic training that I received at Camp Kilmer was easy for me because of B.M.I. I already knew how to march, how to field-strip an M-1 rifle, how to read a map, etc. What was new to me was K.P. (kitchen police) duty. Now that was a trip! I don't know which was worse; cleaning the grease traps, or being assigned to wash the pots and pans. I started to wonder what a college graduate and successful beer salesman was doing in a place like this. One of my fellow soldiers told me how he planned to get out of the army. He pricked his finger and put a couple of drops of blood in the urine sample that was required as part of our frequent physicals. This worked for him. He got a medical discharge, was separated from the service, and I never saw him again. This course of action was not for me. I decided to tough it out and before I knew it the eight weeks of basic training was over and I was sent to Fort Lee, Virginia, to attend another eight weeks of training in the Quartermaster Corps.

The training at Fort Lee was mostly conducted in the classroom. The courses were designed to prepare us for the duties of a supply sergeant. The subjects were fairly simplistic such as typing, inventory control, supply management, etc. It was all I could do to keep from falling asleep during the classroom instruction.

In addition to being assigned K.P. duty occasionally, there were other obnoxious tasks that us buck privates were given. Guard duty was one of them. My first stint at guard duty consisted of protecting a fence during the hours of midnight to 8a.m. in the morning. The only thing that fence did, as far as I was concerned, was to prevent a bunch of cows from encroaching on one of the rifle ranges. Since I was told that the penalty for falling asleep while on guard duty was to face the firing squad, I marched back and forth all night long accompanied by my new friends, the cows.

Another choice duty was serving as a fireman. Coal stoves heated all of the barracks and the fireman's job was to stoke coal and remove the burnt ashes. This delightful job was also conducted at night. Although the penalty for dereliction of duty was not the firing squad, it was worse. It meant facing a bunch of frozen soldiers in the morning with murder in their eyes. I think it was somewhere between the second and third appointment as fireman, that I came to some serious decisions. I decided that I never wanted to march guard again, never wanted to do K.P. again, never wanted to be a fireman again, and definitely had no desire to become a supply sergeant. Because I couldn't quit my job as a soldier, the only solution that I came up with was to become an officer and a gentleman. To that end, I applied for and was accepted at the Infantry Officer Candidate School located at Fort Benning, Georgia.

Part of the acceptance process was to be interviewed by a panel of seven officers, headed up by a lieutenant colonel. The interview started off with the lieutenant colonel asking me, "Why is it that you now want to become an officer when you had a chance to go to West Point or complete your R.O.T.C. training in college?"

"Well sir," I replied. "After six years at a military school, I was kind of tired of that lifestyle and needed some separation from a military environment." That's what I said. What I thought was *You pompous ass should understand that all those crappy assignments you impose on us poor buck privates would make becoming an officer highly desirable.*

One of the captains on the panel asked,

"How can a skinny little private like you expect to withstand the rigors of O.C.S.?" My response was, "I was the champion of my weight class in boxing in college and I'm a lot stronger than I look."

What I thought was, *Why don't you step outside, sir, so I can beat the living crap out of you?!*

The interview lasted an hour and I guess my acting skills prevailed, because they allowed this skinny little private to attend O.C.S, perhaps with the thought that I would probably wash out of the program.

On April 24, 1953, I reported for duty at Fort Benning as an officer candidate. There were two hundred and two of us who reported in that day. We were from all different branches of the army. Some of the soldiers had many years of service and were non-commissioned officers, and some, like me, had only a few months under our belts.

On October 1, 1953, I received my commission as a 2nd Lieutenant, graduating 23rd out of my class that had dwindled down to one hundred and twenty three officer candidates. Forty percent of my class did not make it all the way through the six-month program and were washed out, some of them during the last few days of training. The reason for this high percentage of failure was quite simple. O.C.S. was a living hell and to survive it you had to take everything they threw at you, learn under intense pressure, but most importantly you had to have a burning desire to earn those gold bars. I had been denied this opportunity at Bordentown, and I was determined to be successful at Fort Benning.

On my very first day I learned an invaluable lesson. My Tactical Officer (T. O.), Lt. Fox, said to me at 5p.m. that day,

"Why haven't you shaved?"

I replied, "Sir, Candidate Silberman, sir, I shaved at 5a.m. when we got up for reveille and I have a fast-growing beard and it's probably just five o'clock shadow."

"That's no excuse Candidate Silberman. Now tell me why you haven't shaved?"

"Sir, Candidate Silberman, sir, there is no excuse, sir."

We were responsible for our actions and there never was an excuse for anything that we did or said. I carried a disposable razor in my boot from that day forth and whenever we had a ten-minute break, I would dry-shave myself and was never accused of not shaving again.

One of the lasting impressions I have about O.C.S is how arduous the physical conditioning was, especially during the first eight weeks of training. Before breakfast, and after we had cleaned up our barracks for inspection, we would form as a company for physical exercise which consisted of doing the "daily dozen." This was a series of twelve exercises and each day the number of repetitions of each exercise was increased. After that torture session was completed, we would double-time (run) to the mess hall for our breakfast. There was still one last act of torture before breakfast. There was a chin-up bar located in front of the mess hall door and we would have to do chin-ups before being allowed to enter. The first day we had to do ten chin-ups and each day we had to do more until the limit was set at fifty. That wasn't all. While we were doing our exercises the five Tactical Officers (T.O's) assigned to our company would be yelling and screaming at us to get it right.

"Candidate Silberman, you are not going all the way down with that push-up!"

"Sorry sir."

"Sorry, my ass, give me ten more!"

"Yes, sir."

"Candidate Silberman, if you ever want breakfast, you better get that stupid chin of yours over the bar!"

"Sorry sir."

"Sorry, my ass, give me five more!"

Finally breakfast and then back to the barracks for inspection.

During those first weeks, there was hardly any time for ourselves except for the four or five hours of sleep we got at night. In the evening, in order to prepare for the morning's inspection, we had to wash the windows, wax the floors, shine our boots, and clean our weapons, in addition to any homework that was assigned us. Our floors were so highly polished that if we walked on them, they would get scuffmarks so we would either take our boots off or wear little booties that covered them.

There were all kinds of inspections. Sometimes we were required to stand at attention for three hours in the blistering Georgia sun for rifle inspection. Several candidates fainted and were carted away to the infirmary, never to be seen again. There were footlocker inspections.

"Fall out of ranks, open your footlockers and join ranks again in sixty seconds!"

There were pack inspections, patch inspections, haircut inspections, fingernail inspections, shave inspections, foot inspections, etc. All of these inspections were conducted either by our T.O's or by the candidates in blue helmets. If you survived the first twenty weeks of O.C.S. you were given a blue helmet (Blue Beetle) and now could harass the officer candidates from different companies who were junior to you. These blue beetles demanded respect and they got it.

"Brace yourself, Candidate Silberman!"

A brace was not a tooth-straightening devise, but a back straightening torture.

Then there was the "Run." We would start out slowly, just marching down a road with our backpacks on and our rifles in hand. The command would come "Double Time March" and the fun would begin. Sweat would ooze from every pore in my body and I would watch the neck of the candidate running in front of me turn from pink to bright red.

"Third platoon, pass the first and second platoon and take the lead!"

"Second platoon, pass the first platoon and third platoon, and take the lead!"

And so on, mile after torturous mile. More candidates broke ranks, fell to the side of the road vomiting, were driven to the infirmary, and washed out of O.C.S.

Toward the end of the first eight weeks, as the resignations trickled in and the washouts slowed down, a pattern was forming and everything began to fall into place. We began to recognize each other as individuals and not just officer candidates. I became "Silby" to my friends in the company as opposed to always being referred to as "Candidate Silberman." We started to recognize who was good at what, and who needed help. We started to bond with each other and came to recognize that integrity was an indispensable ingredient of leadership.

Now, the classroom instruction intensified. First we were instructed how to fire all kinds of weapons, The M-1 rifle gave way to the B.A.R. (Browning Automatic Rifle), which was followed by various types of machine guns.

"Candidate Silberman?"

"Sir, Candidate Silberman."

"Candidate, will you tell the class in a loud clear voice how the disconnector spring housing group cams with the trigger guard, and why this is an extra safety precaution?"

"It clicks once, sir. This won't let it fire."

"Thank you, Candidate Silberman."

The days wore on with plain rifles, night firing rifles, machine guns, 57 millimeter mortars, 81 millimeter mortars, 4.2 mortars; assembly and disassembly, techniques of firing, and combat applications. All of this instruction was followed by written tests, oral tests, and practical tests. Simultaneously, we were given instruction in leadership and command, and administrative courses such as personnel problems and company paperwork.

Spring turned into the hot Georgia summer that boiled the water in our canteens and baked the backs of our necks on the various rifle ranges. It made our afternoon P. T. (physical training) test a nightmare with all of us candidates swimming in our own sweat.

" Candidate Silberman, you owe it to yourself to do the best that you can!"

"Yes sir, Lieutenant."

Next came instruction in hand-to-hand combat. We were paired up alphabetically so my partner for combat instruction was candidate Neil P. Shanahan, a two-hundred pound Irishman from Pennsylvania.

"OK, Candidate Silberman, using the techniques you just learned, heave candidate Shanahan over your left shoulder!"

"Yes, sir!"

"You skinny little shit, you'll never be able to toss me!"

"Watch your mouth, Shan and over you go!"

When I graduated from O.C.S, I weighed all of 113 pounds, which probably was a record at Fort Benning. Shanahan used to say as a compliment to me that I was "a hundred and thirteen pounds of romping, stomping shit."

The next torture in store for us was the obstacle course. One of the obstacles was a thirty-foot wall with netting over it that we had to climb up hand over hand and when we reached the top we had to leap off into a pile of sawdust.

"Candidate Silberman, you have three minutes to get up and over"

"Yes. Sir."

Since I have a fear of heights, I knew that when I mastered this obstacle I could do anything. There were many other obstacles on the course, equally difficult; practically all of us made it safely through and only a couple of candidates washed out because of it. None of us regretted mastering the obstacle course, because it was one more torture never to be repeated.

After a couple of weeks of classroom instruction which dealt with the functions of the S-1, S-2, S-3, and S-4, we moved on to Tactics. Each subject was followed by a graded test and the biggest test of all was to stay awake and pay attention.

"Candidate Silberman, open your eyes and listen!"

"Yes, sir, Lieutenant!"

Tactics consisted of two weeks of utter hell in the broiling Georgia summer. I had to run up and down hills lugging a machine gun, 57 Millimeter recoil-less rifle, or an M-1. There were problems of all sorts that we had to solve.

"Candidate Silberman, where would you place the 50 caliber machine gun if the enemy is approaching from the south?"

All of the problems had textbook solutions but the common thread was exhaustion. But in those two weeks, I learned a lot about myself. I learned that I could lead a platoon of forty-four men in a variety of defensive or offensive maneuvers without disaster. I leaned what our motto "Follow Me" meant.

The end was in sight. I was given my blue helmet (Blue Beetle) and I had the first taste of rank and privilege as well as responsibility. I started to think that I might actually graduate and have those beautiful gold bars pinned to my uniform. There was just one last hurdle before graduation day, October 1st, 1953. This was the dreaded "Seventy-two Hour Test." We marched nine miles out to the bivouac area where the fun and games began. This was three solid days of non-stop action. The T.O's would assign us duties based on the weaknesses they had discovered in us during the past many months.

"Candidate Silberman, for the first twenty-four hours of the attack drill, you will be the machine gunner!"

"Yes, sir."

Since I had proven myself as a leader, I was not given any command positions during the three-day period but only assignments designed to wear me out physically

"OK, Candidate Silberman, start humping that 57 recoilless rifle, while we set up a defensive perimeter."

"Yes sir." (That son of a bitch weighs more than I do!)

And so it went for the entire seventy-two hours with sleep coming in ten-minute snatches. As hard as they tried, they could not break me, although a few of my fellow candidates washed out for making bad command decisions during this final test. I guess that if it were a real combat situation, their decisions would have cost the lives of the men they were leading.

At last, it was over. We were given a forty-eight hour pass to go into town to buy our new officer uniforms. One of the privileges of rank was that we had to buy our own uniforms while as enlisted men they were supplied to us. In addition to buying all the required uniforms, I also bought a brand new car, a 1953 Studebaker, for $2,300.00. This beautiful car was red and white with a white leather interior and was the first of many cars that I would buy.

October 1st finally arrived and I, along with one hundred and twenty two others, received our commissions as 2nd Lieutenants. Lt. Fox, my T.O. pinned the gold bars on me and said,

"Congratulations, John. I knew you could make it and please call me John."

"Yes sir, Lt. Fox, sir."

He was my God and my mentor.

"You can do better, Candidate Silberman!"

"You owe it to yourself to try harder, Candidate Silberman!"

"You can run faster, Candidate Silberman!"

He was the devil and my chief torturer.

"Drop down and give me twenty more, Candidate Silberman!"

"There is a speck of rust in your rifle, Candidate Silberman. You are confined to quarters for the weekend!"

"I cannot see my reflection on the shine of your boots, Candidate Silberman. You are confined to quarters for the weekend!"

He was Lt. Fox. He was my Tactical Officer, and always would be. He could never ever be John Fox, my friend. And so it was. I went to O.C.S. as a happy-go-lucky college kid and came out as a "lean, mean, killing machine," or as Lt. Shanahan said, "one hundred and thirteen pounds of romping, stomping shit!"

My next post was Aberdeen Proving Grounds located in Aberdeen, Maryland. The Army had enough Infantry Second Lieutenants at that time so I, and several other members of my O.C.S class, were sent to Aberdeen to become Ordnance Officers.

Since the training program did not begin for several weeks, I was given command of a basic training company. Yippee! My first command, and I was going to show those soldiers a thing or two.

"First Sergeant, form the company at five AM and we'll go for a little run."

"Sir, these soldiers have only been in the army for four weeks and they are not in shape to do any running!"

"Never mind, Sergeant, do as I say!"

"Yes, sir, Lieutenant Silberman.

In the afternoon, prior to "The Run," I reconnoitered a five- mile stretch on the base that would be a perfect training ground for my soldiers. Five AM finally came and my company was formed, as ordered. "Soldiers," I said. "We will double-time for five miles, return to base and then do ten repetitions of the 'daily dozen' and then you may have breakfast."

"Follow me!" and I started to double-time. After about a mile, I turned around to see how my boys were doing and discovered there was nobody behind me except for my first sergeant.

"I told you sir, that these soldiers were too new to be doing any running and about several hundred yards into the run they started to break ranks and become sick by the side of the road. I had my platoon sergeants walk them back to their barracks, sir."

"We'll see about that, first sergeant!"

When I got back to my company headquarters, there was a message that my battalion commander wanted to see me forthwith.

" Lt. Silberman, reporting as ordered, sir."

"You Goddamn 90-day wonder." (Actually I was a 180-day wonder). "What the hell do you think you were doing, taking those 4-F soldiers out for a run even before the sun is up? These soldiers are going to be trained to fix jeeps and tanks, and the like, and are not going to see any combat. Now, you let the sergeants run the company and if you pull any more stupid tricks like you did this morning, I'll have your ass for grass. Now get the hell out of here!"

"Yes, sir."

"First Sergeant, if you need me you can find me either at the officers' club or in my room at the BOQ (Bachelor Officers Quarters)."

Hell, if the major wanted the sergeants to run my company, so be it. I soon discovered during an extensive happy hour at the Club, that Martinis were ten cents a pop. I would load up, and some of my new buddies and I would pile into my car and head into Baltimore to visit the numerous strip joints and other dens of iniquity that East Fourth Street had to offer. This lasted for about four weeks until my classes in Ordnance began. I actually put back on twenty of the pounds that I had sweated off during the summer at O.C.S.

My work ethic returned. The classes were very difficult for me and I had to spend a lot of time studying in order to pass the exams. I am not very mechanical and learning the workings of the internal combustion engine and actually disassembling and reassembling them did not come easy to me. I prevailed, however, and was awarded the "Flaming Piss Pots" as the insignia of an Ordinance Officer. This was in exchange for the Crossed Rifles insignia of an Infantry Officer.

As luck would have it, all the officers in the Ordnance program were assigned their new stations alphabetically. Lt's Shanahan and above were assigned to Europe. Lt's Silberman and below were assigned to Korea.

"It's just the luck of the Irish," Shanahan said to me.

"Fuck off, Shan, before I toss you over my left shoulder again!"

I was given two weeks leave in order to get my affairs in order before I began the long trek to Korea. The most important task that I had to accomplish was to see that my beautiful Studebaker was cared for during my absence. My sister had some friends who lived on Long Island, New York, who agreed to keep my car up on blocks in their garage. Since I did not have a girlfriend to kiss goodbye, I spent the rest of my leave drinking with my buddies and listening to jazz at the various nightspots in Greenwich Village and on 52nd Street in Manhattan.

I received orders to travel by train to Camp Stoneham in California. The train was civilian but the army commandeered four cars to transport troops from the East Coast to the West Coast. Since I was an officer, I was given a sleeping berth and was placed in command of one of the troop cars.

" Hey, Loot, do you want to join us guys in a friendly game of poker?

I had been taught not to fraternize with enlisted men as "familiarity breeds contempt."

"Sure boys, how about five card stud, three raise limit with 50 cents to a buck per bet?'

"You're on Lieutenant, deal!"

It took two nights and three days to arrive in California but I arrived $500.00 richer than when I began.

"Thank you, boys."

I had never been in California before, and I absolutely fell in love with San Francisco. I had several days before my flight to Tokyo and I took full advantage of this time by exploring the city. One of the things that impressed me was that unlike NYC, the streets were very clean. I also took a tour through Golden Gate Park and visited the DeYoung museum. The park was drop-dead gorgeous and the museum had incredible exhibits. And naturally, I spent time at the various bars and restaurants at Fisherman's Wharf, which in those days was a working fishing port, and not the tourist trap that it is now.

Unlike the Vietnam era, during the Korean War, men in uniform were respected by civilians, and were shown great courtesy.

"Lieutenant, where are you from?"

"New York City, sir"

"Are you being sent to Korea, son?"

"Yes sir, I am."

"Well, you are a long way from home. How would you like to come home with me and meet the wife and kids and have a nice home cooked meal?"

"I'd love it. Thank you very much, sir!"

I swore that someday I would live in California and eight years later I did.

After falling in love with San Francisco, it was now time to leave it and head on to Japan and ultimately to Korea. Transportation to

Japan was by way of an old cargo plane that made stops in Hawaii and Wake Island before arriving in Tokyo. It was a horrible trip, being strapped into a small seat with a parachute on my back and a carbine weapon in my lap. To make things worse, several of the troops that I was in charge of got sick and threw up all over the plane.

The day after I arrived in Tokyo, I was sent by boat to a small island, Etta Jima, where for three weeks I learned about C.B.R. (Chemical, Biological, and Radiological warfare.) We had the stuff back then and so did our enemies the North Koreans and Chinese. It is interesting to note that our current President, George W. Bush wants to knock off Saddam Hussein for having "weapons of mass destruction" when that crap has been around for over fifty years.

At any rate, as soon as we arrived at the army base on the island, the colonel in charge gave us an orientation lecture.

"You new officers want to be aware of two dangers on this island during your three-week stay here. The first is, all the prostitutes over here have the clap and you don't want to mess with them. Secondly, there are a lot of card sharks here and you don't want to lose your hard-earned pay. Got it, boys?"

"Yes. Sir!"

That evening, at the Officer's Club, our colonel was sitting at a round poker table.

" Come on boys, sit over here for a friendly game of seven-card stud."

He solved both problems for us since he took our money before the card sharks could get to us and we had no money for the prostitutes with clap!

After completing the C.B.R. training I was shipped back to a Repo Depot (Replacement Depot) at Camp Drake in Tokyo. I was to be assigned to the 707 Ordinance Battalion of the Second Infantry Division in Korea. I had a few days to myself before flying to Korea, and I spent the time exploring what Tokyo had to offer. The exchange rate was 360 yen to the dollar so everything was incredibly cheap. I bought a German make Zeiss Icon 35 millimeter camera for about

$25.00. I also bought my sister a real pearl necklace for under $100.00

The streets of Tokyo were crowded and the people, although courteous, still bore some resentment against Americans for having used atomic bombs against them in World War Two. Unlike what I was about to discover in Korea, the Japanese people were extremely clean and would bathe several times a day. They had public bathhouses where for a few yen you could bathe in a coed environment. This brought back memories of my experiences at the nudist colony in New Jersey.

All good things must end. I was finally ordered to Korea where I would spend the next thirteen months of my life in an environment that was nasty beyond belief.

I arrived in Seoul and was immediately put in the back of a four-by-four truck destined for the town of Weejambo near what was to become the D.M.Z. (demilitarized zone). The truck ride was over a dirt road and opened my eyes to the sight of Papa-Sans and Mama-Sans trudging by the side of the rode laden with an A-frame like contraption that held large buckets on each side. My nose became alerted to the contents of those buckets. They contained human excrement that the Koreans used to fertilize their rice paddies. The stench was further exacerbated by the stink of *Kimchi*, which was the rotten cabbage dish that the Koreans ate for lunch and dinner. I finally arrived at the Seventh Division and was given a Wheeled Vehicle Repair platoon to command. My Platoon Sergeant, Sergeant Allen, a giant of a man from Alabama, formed my platoon.

"This here is Lieutenant Silberman, fresh over from the States. Now, we all know that he probably don't know shit, but y'all do what he says, or I'll kick your asses, one by one!"

After that wonderful introduction to the soldiers that I would be responsible for during the next thirteen months, I had the pleasure of meeting my Company Commander.

"Lieutenant Silberman, reporting for duty, sir."

"Sit down Silberman and get a load off your feet. I just got me a new supply of magazines that I'll share with you. Get a load of this one. Did you ever see anything like that before? I reckon she's a five pounder!" Have a drink, Silberman! There's some gin in that glass."

"Thank you, sir. I think I will!"

This career army creep of a captain had a stack of girly magazines, (this was before Playboy and Hustler) which consisted of pictures of girls in their underwear. This sorry excuse for an officer was drunk as a skunk and would remain drunk until they shipped his sorry ass back to the States some few months later. This sick son of a bitch had some mysterious rating system that classified the girls as either one, two, three, four, or five pounders. I never found out which was best, one or five.

Being in command of a Wheel Vehicle Repair platoon was similar to being in charge of the service department of an automobile dealership. Sergeant Allen, acting as a foreman, saw to it that the work was done and my job was to schedule the repairs, order the supplies and parts, and provide leadership over the entire operation. A cease-fire had been declared so that we were in no danger of being killed by the North Koreans or Chinese. Our biggest enemy was the weather.

I have never been so cold in my life as I was during that winter in Korea. Since I was an officer, I lived in a small tent all by myself whereas my troops lived in tents that housed about fifteen soldiers. Small gas-operated furnaces that frequently extinguished themselves at night heated the tents.

"Sergeant Allen, get someone the fuck up here right now to light my furnace. I'm freezing my ass off!"

It was so cold that the water in my five-gallon can would turn to solid ice. That was not a good thing. I needed the water from that can to shave and bathe. We would pour water into our steel helmets, heat the water with a small can of Sterno, and then go about the business of shaving and cleaning ourselves. About once a month we were permitted to go back to headquarters where we could indulge in the luxury of a shower and a hot meal.

Mostly what we ate while in the field were "C" rations that for the most part tasted like shit. Once in a while, I was able to trade a surplus jeep to one of the Quartermaster outfits that I supported for a case of frozen steaks.

"Come on boys, let's get a fire going and eat something good, for a change. Corporal, get that case of beer that I saw you smuggle into your tent this morning and we'll have that with our steaks!"

Time went by and finally my thirteen-month stint in Korea came to an end. My battalion commander said, "John, you've done a fine job running that platoon of yours. I'd like you to consider signing up for another four years and I'll guarantee you a tour in Europe."

"Thank you, sir, but I think not. I've enjoyed working for you, but I need to get on with the rest of my life."

"OK, son, good luck to you and watch out for those civilians!"

My flight out of the Orient was much pleasanter than my arrival. We were flown out of Korea on a commercial flight with honest to goodness American stewardesses. Not having seen an attractive woman for all those months, they were a sight for sore eyes.

"Hi, sweetie. How about letting me buy you a fine dinner when we hit San Francisco? I'll even pop for a show!"

"In your dreams, Lieutenant."

I knew I was heading home. I separated from the service on March 22, 1955 and a new chapter in my life was to about to begin and a new chapter in the book is about to begin.

Chapter Five
Work, Law School, Love and Marriage

1955 - 1961

Re-entry to civilian life was difficult and painful for me. In the army I knew who I was. I was Lt. Silberman, a platoon leader, an officer and gentleman, a leader, respected, and respectful. The organization was clear. I knew where I fit and where everyone else belonged. There was no guessing. A lieutenant was higher than a sergeant and lower than a captain. There were rules for everything. Reveille to wake you up and taps to put you to sleep. The path to command was clear. You would be promoted to captain, to major, to colonel, to general if you played by the rules, weren't killed, and were patient.

Back home, living again with my mother, I was hearing,

"Johnny, why are you smoking so much?"

"Johnny, when are you going to get a real job?"

"Johnny, when are you going to start law school?

"Johnny, have you been drinking again?"

I felt lost. I had no identity. I was not John, the college student. I was not John, the beer salesman. I was not John, the soldier. I became John the nothing. All the confidence that I had acquired over the years was leaching from my soul. I started to walk miles through the streets of Manhattan searching for some clue as to who I was and what I was to become. I became disillusioned, angry, and depressed. I avoided my friends and was rude to my mother who had no comprehension of what I was feeling. I started to drink heavily. I forgot how to smile.

One evening after about a month of wandering around, I wound up at the Dover Bar on Lexington Avenue and 78th street. I listened to a conversation at the bar that two men were having. They were talking about the joys of being in advertising and how their skills caused people to buy things they really didn't need. I heard them bragging about their ability to put subliminal messages in radio spots that would convince the audience of the purity of their products. That conversation focused me on what I did not want to become; people like them.

After many Scotches and a great deal of soul searching, it suddenly dawned on me what direction my life needed to take. I would utilize my leadership and sales skills and become a chief executive of a major corporation. With this new focus in life, and purpose replacing desperation, I began to apply for jobs at major US corporations. I straightened up my act, cut back on drinking, and finally began adjusting to life as a civilian. I could smile again. I soon received a letter that would start me on a career that would last for almost fifty years.

May 18, 1955

John K. Silberman
969 Park Avenue
New York, New York

Dear Mr. Silberman:

This is to advise you that you have been favorably considered for acceptance into the Management Training Program of Curtiss-Wright Corporation's Wright Aeronautical Division.
Your selection for this program was made after extensive

deliberation which involved a careful study of your qualifications in relation to those of the very large number of young men who applied.

The company greatly appreciates the forbearance, which you have shown during this selection period.

I am sure that your decision to join us will result in a long and profitable association for both the company and yourself.

Very truly yours,
(signed)

Robert G. Conrad
Training Manager

"Hey Mom! I just got a job offer to go to work for the Curtiss-Wright Company as a management trainee. Isn't that great?

"What about law school? I thought that you promised to go to law school. You must become a lawyer!" her voice, always harsh, shrieked.

I thought about strangling her. Here I am, ex-army officer, out of the service for only two months, and yet she is treating me like a little boy that has to be told what to do. But there was no use arguing with her.

"OK, Mom. I'll apply for the evening law school at N.Y.U. If I'm accepted, I'll work during the day and go to law school at night."

"That's a good boy, Johnny!"

I started working at Curtiss-Wright that summer, 1955. Of the twelve management trainees that started, ten of us completed the 18-month program. We were told that we were selected for the program out of over a thousand applicants, which made us feel pretty special. We were a very diverse group. The only common thread was that each of us had served in the military in some type of leadership capacity. We discovered that Bob Conrad was an ex-West Pointer; that explained his selection criterion. The starting salary for each of us was $75.00 a week, which in 1955 was a decent wage.

I thoroughly enjoyed the management-training program. Once again I was part of a group and had new friends with whom I would share many common experiences. The training consisted of three phases: classroom instruction, shop, and work place internships.

The classroom instruction was like being back in college except there were far fewer students. The subjects all involved principles of management. We all had huge egos that led to some pretty lively discussions and debates. However, since we were all college graduates, the instruction soon became boring and we looked forward to the shop phase.

Curtiss-Wright manufactured both reciprocating and jet engines. It was believed that as future managers, we would be better equipped to lead if we understood the machinery that was used to manufacture those engines. This phase of the program lasted six months, which I felt was five months too long. We learned how to read blueprints and operate all types of machines from simple lathes to complex milling machines. Not being a mechanical person, this part of the program was not easy for me. I did manage to survive unscathed, although one of my fellow trainees, Stan Vitt, managed to lose part of his index finger to a drill bit.

Because of the constant nagging of my mother, I applied for, and was accepted, at the evening division of the New York School of Law. So, in addition to having a full time job, I now saddled myself with having to go to law school four nights a week for four long years. My good friend, Bob Davidson, was also accepted, but had the good sense to quit after the first semester.

I look back on those days and wonder how the hell I managed. I would get up at 6 a.m. and have breakfast. On good days it would take me about an hour to drive from Manhattan to Wood-Ridge where Curtiss-Wright was located. In the winter, when it was snowing, it would sometimes take about two hours to get to work. After work, I would drive back to Manhattan and slowly circle around the law school until I could find a parking spot where I could leave my car. After classes were over, at about 10p.m., I would get back in the car and drive home. I would have to repeat the circling process in order to find a parking spot where I could leave my car overnight. It was now about 11p.m. I would fix myself something to eat and prepare to study for the next three hours in addition to any work-related projects that needed to be accomplished. I would fall into bed around 2 or 3 a.m. only to wake up at 6a.m. to repeat the process all over again. I must have been crazy!

One of the most enjoyable parts of being a management trainee was being assigned to a variety of departments. I had a three-month stint with the personnel department where I conducted interviews, assisted in resolving labor disputes, and wrote personnel policies. Another nifty job was my assignment to the planning department. I was assigned to a team responsible for the planning and acquisition of an IBM Model 650. This machine was the most powerful computer of its day but now could not hold a torch to a simple desktop model and is probably in the Smithsonian museum. This was my first exposure to the world of Information Technology that became my life's work.

The frantic pace of work and school left no time for a social life so when Stan Vitt suggested that we share a place for the summer of 1956, I jumped at the opportunity. We found a nice cottage at Greenwood Lake that was located in both New Jersey and New York States. The rent for the cottage included a boat that we called our yacht, but in reality was a small rowboat with an outboard engine.

That summer was one of the best times ever. I had a job that I liked. I had associates that I admired. I had a roommate with whom I was compatible. I did not have to go to school at night, and I met the love of my life.

When Stan and I came home from work, we would change into swimsuits and take our yacht for a spin. We would take a swim, go back to our cottage, and get dressed for the evening. Stan, a very good cook, would occasionally fix dinner for the two of us, but on most nights we would go to the Linden House to eat. After dinner we would belly-up to the bar and invite whatever girls were there to talk or dance with us.

One Saturday night, early in the summer, we met four girls who also had a cottage at the Lake, but they only came up for weekends. They all worked in New York City and it was too long a commute to come up on a daily basis. One of the girls, Rita, invited the two of us to meet them at their cottage the following Saturday for a spaghetti feast. I started to chat with Barbara Birmingham, a blue-eyed, blonde beauty. We talked for a while and had a few drinks and then we danced. That's all it took. I fell madly in love with her and could hardly wait for the next weekend to arrive.

As my summer romance with Barbara progressed, my relationship with Stan started to flounder. During the week we continued our routine of boating, swimming and going to the Linden House. The problem was that Stan was interested in picking up girls at the bar and I wasn't.

"Gee whiz, John. I took those two girls we were talking to for a ride in my car and if you had come along we would have made out like bandits!"

"I told you, Stan, I'm not interested. Barbara is coming up Friday night and that's all I care about."

Barbara and her roommates would arrive on Friday evenings, and on many Saturdays, some, if not all, of my fellow trainees would arrive for the weekend. It would be party, party, party all weekend long! We would drink case after case of beer, especially the beer that had trivia questions printed on the cans. We would go boating, swim, tell jokes, neck, and all in all have a marvelous time

One weekend, Barbara invited her mother Florence (Nina) to come join the fun. On Saturday we all went swimming. Barbara, a strong swimmer, decided that she would swim across the lake and back. Naturally, Nina got nervous because the lake was quite wide where Barbara had decided to swim.

"Bobbie, I think it's too far to go and I don't think you should try."

"Oh Mom, I'm a good swimmer and I won't have any problem making it across and back!"

"Not to worry, Nina," I said. "If she gets into trouble, I'll save her."

"Go ahead, dear, as long as John is here if you need him, I won't worry anymore."

The truth of the matter is that I can barely "dog paddle" and for me to swim across the lake would be impossible. I was trying to impress Barbara's mother and I succeeded. To her dying day, she never knew that I tricked her on the very first day that I met her. At any rate, Bobbie completed the swim without any problems and earned a congratulatory kiss from me for her success.

Stan's parents were invited up for a weekend visit. Stan and I were a little apprehensive about the visit since his parents were teetotalers and we knew there would be a lot of beer guzzling going on. We needn't have worried. They arrived with a large watermelon that they punctured with an ice pick. They poured a fifth of Vodka into the watermelon and the next day they cut it up and started to eat impressive slices of the melon. Pretty soon they joined us in our weekend festivities of joke-telling, trivia games, and all around merriment. We learned that teetotalers were allowed to eat watermelon.

The summer was quickly coming to an end. I dreaded the thought of returning to my mother's apartment and having to begin my second year of law school. The only bright spot was having met Bobbie and knowing that I would continue to see her in the future. Summer romances normally end in the fall or result in marriage. On our last weekend at Greenwood Lake we were having drinks at the Lone Pine Inn.

"Bobbie what do you think our folks are going to think about us going out together with you being Irish Catholic and me being Jewish?"

"I don't think it's going to be a problem. My mother adores you and I have a sister who is married to a guy who is half Jewish although the family keeps it a secret because his sister is married to an anti-Semite. My other sister is married to a bigot, but I hate him and his opinion means nothing to me. What about your family?"

"My dad will love you on first sight. His second wife, Ida, was an Irish-Catholic girl who converted to Judaism in order to marry my dad. There will be no problem in that department but my mother is another story. She hates anyone who is not Jewish so I can't count on her liking you at all."

We continued to talk about what our religions meant to each other. Being Jewish meant nothing to me and while Bobbie was a Catholic she had absolutely no prejudices whatsoever. While we were having this serious discussion, an asshole a few bar stools away was telling his buddy that the Jews were responsible for all the world's troubles and that Hitler had the right idea. Instead of going over and decking the asshole like I would normally do, I told Bobbie that if she married me she would have to put up with this verbal abuse all of her life. She said that she had heard worse and that the world was full of assholes like this guy and not to worry about it and that she could handle it.

I told her that I loved her and wanted to marry her and she said yes. We decided not to get married until the spring of the next year, 1957, so that I could complete my second year of law school, finish my training program, and get a real job at Curtis-Wright.

The summer was over and I moved back into my mother's apartment in Manhattan and Bobbie went back to her mother's apartment in Brooklyn. My life was even more hectic than the year before. Not only did I have work and law school to contend with, but after I got home from school, Bobbie and I would talk on the phone for hours. On weekends I would drive through the Brooklyn Battery Tunnel and go to her apartment, ostensibly to study. If her mother wasn't home, the studying would go out the window and we would neck and make plans for our future life together.

One of the decisions that we made was that we would get married in the Catholic Church. This was an easy decision for me to make. Religion meant nothing to me and Nina wanted her youngest daughter to be married in a church because her two older daughters were married in civil ceremonies. In order for a non-Catholic to be married in church a course of instruction was required. Something else I had to fit into an excruciatingly busy schedule. I met a really nice young priest who scheduled three training sessions for me. Rather than learn about the mysteries of the Catholic faith, we mainly talked about baseball and politics. The only thing that came close to religious instruction was that I learned that I had to sign a document where I would promise to raise any children that were born to us in the Catholic faith. Again, I had no problem with that requirement. I was ill equipped to bring up my kids in the Jewish faith because I knew so little about it.

During our engagement I met Bobbie's family. I already knew her mother from our Greenwood Lake days. Her two older sisters (one 17 years older and the other 14 years older), both lived in Levittown on Long Island. Florrie, the older of the two, was married to a wonderful guy, Dave Cardoza. Dave was a self-made man. For his entire career he worked for the Federal Government. He started as a messenger in the Customs Agency and when he retired he was Commissioner of Customs, the highest position obtainable. When I first met the Cardozas, their children, Donnie and Carolee, were very young and extremely cute.

Bobbie's other sister, Fran was married to Eddie Rudolph, one of the biggest assholes I had ever met. He was a liar, thief, molester, and a generally repugnant individual. His only saving grace was that he was extremely handsome which is what probably attracted Fran to him in the first place. When I met them they had one child, Linda, who unfortunately had spina bifida and remained dependent on crutches for her whole life.

Bobbie's family was very accepting of me with the possible exception of Eddie. Fla and Dave would invite the family out to their house for an evening of eating, drinking, and singing. The girls, including Nina, sang beautifully and Dave had a nice voice as well. I couldn't sing a note but I had a great time listening. Now, not only did I have Bobbie, but I had future in-laws that were fun to be with.

When I introduced Bobbie to my family, I was apprehensive. I needn't have been. As I had anticipated, my father and Ida welcomed her with open arms. My half-brother, Bill, who is ten years younger than I am, fell in love with her instantly. My mother was a little cooler, but welcomed her nonetheless. My mother's only advice to me was that I should always be good to her. My sister and her husband, Todd, also were very welcoming and Pat and Bobbie became fast friends and still are.

In January of that year, 1957, I completed the Management

Training Program and was assigned to the Industrial Engineering Department. My job was to conduct a cost/benefit analysis for any items that the various departments wanted to purchase. My salary was increased to $150.00 a week so I was in the chips.

I soon became bored with this work as it was excruciatingly dull. There was very little personal interaction and the job consisted mainly of detailed financial analysis. I soon became exposed to the reality of corporate politics. The department was headed by Bill, an ex army general, who, we believed, was hired because of his military contacts. Bill had two Section Chiefs reporting to him, Shelly and Stan.

Stan was my boss, and one day he called me into his office and said:

"John, in order to be successful at Curtiss-Wright, and climb the corporate ladder, you need to join the Management Club, and I will sponsor you."

"Stan, I am currently working over forty hours a week, going to law school four nights a week, and am planning for my wedding in May. I don't have any spare time to spend joining any clubs. Anyway, why did I just spend 18 months going through the company training program, if I wasn't destined for management?"

"You really are pretty naive, John. The only reason the company has the training program is because we do so much business with the military and they insist on our having such a program. Believe me, the only way to achieve success here is to join the Management Club and make those important contacts with your superiors."

"Now you tell me! But it doesn't matter because I'm not joining, period."

Crossing my boss was not the smartest thing that I did. He started to nit-pick my cost/benefit analyses and arranged to have me transferred to another group that was responsible for writing policies and procedures. He was still my boss but I'm sure he knew that this boring assignment would drive me up the wall, and it did. I only had this assignment for a few months when one of my fellow trainees and good friend, Frank Cleary, accepted a job at Aerojet General Corporation in Sacramento, California. Frank arranged for me to get his old job as budget manager for the Spare Parts Department. My new boss, Bob Wadden, also started to encourage me to join the Management Club. Having learned my lesson from Stan, I agreed to join but told Bob that I needed to finish my second year of law school first. Of course, I never did become a member of the Management Club.

Bobbie and I got married in Our Lady of Angels Catholic Church on May 30, 1957. My young brother, Bill, was my best man and prior to the ceremony, Eddie Rudolph, bought us celebratory drinks at a bar close to the church. Eddie managed to get my brother half loaded and when it came time to produce the ring during the ceremony, he had a hard time finding it.

The bride and groom got to the church on time but our priest, Father McKenna, was late. Bobbie cried throughout the entire wedding and when it came time for me to put the ring on her finger after my brother finally found it, I attempted to put it on the ring finger of her right hand. We made it through the rest of the ceremony without any further mishaps and went to Nina's apartment for a family reception. My father had warned us that my mother would never set foot in a Catholic church. However, she fooled us by agreeing to attend and because of that we could not invite Ida to the wedding for fear of an ugly scene. Instead we sent Ida flowers as a form of apology. We had a great time at the reception and my mother and father were cordial to each other.

We spent our wedding night in the bridal suite at the Motel On The Mountain in New Jersey and the next day flew to Saint Thomas in the Virgin Islands for our honeymoon trip. We flew from New York to Puerto Rico on a DC-6 and then changed planes to a DC-3 for the short flight to Saint Thomas.

What a glorious week that was! We had a beautiful room in the Virgin Island Hotel that was located on top of a hill overlooking the town of Charlotte Amalie. In the afternoons we would literally have to push goats out of the way on our stroll into town. Once in town, we did a little shopping with some of the money that was given to us as presents for our wedding. Back then, the only cruise ship that visited Saint Thomas came in every Tuesday, and there were just a few shops and restaurants available. We did manage to find a shop that sold fine china and linens. For the $100.00 that Fla and Dave had given us, we bought a French Limoges service for eight, which we still have after all these years and countless moves around the country.

After a couple of days, and much to our surprise, Howard and Millie, and Morty and Alberta arrived on the scene. These people were friends of Bob Davidson, and both couples were married a few days after we were. Although we had known Howard and Millie previously, Morty and Alberta were new to us. We started to hang out with them and had a great time. On one memorable afternoon, we were all having drinks at an open-air club, and Bobbie got up to sing with the band. She'd had just enough to drink to overcome her innate shyness and sang so beautifully that the patrons kept asking for just one more song.

Our wonderful honeymoon was drawing to a close. We had one last adventure before returning to New York City and a life full of work and school. We flew back from Saint Thomas to Puerto Rico. Our plane from Puerto Rico to New York was not going to leave for about eight hours so we had some time to kill. It was hot as hell and the only places that were air-conditioned back then were the movie houses. Bobbie and I decided to get out of the heat and see a movie. They first showed some cartoons that were really funny with the little animals speaking Spanish. At about the time they started to show the main feature, Bobbie had to go to the bathroom. A few minutes later she came charging back to her seat and grabbed my arm.

"We have to get out of here right now!"

"Are you crazy? They just started the movie and I want to see it. Besides which, it is hot out there."

"I'm leaving and I want you to come right now!"

"OK," is what I said, but what I thought was that the honeymoon was over.

Once outside the theatre she explained that when she went into the bathroom the lights were off. When she turned them on a million cockroaches started scampering around the room. It was the first time that I learned of her complete distaste for the little buggers. We managed to amuse ourselves for the rest of the afternoon and caught the late flight back to New York.

A few weeks before we got married, we rented an apartment at 41 West 88th street in Manhattan. The building that housed our apartment was a newly converted brownstone, divided into ten apartments, two to a floor. We rented the back apartment on the ground floor. It consisted of a large (20 ft. X20 ft.) living room, a tiny bedroom, a small kitchen, and one bathroom. The thing that attracted us to this particular apartment was that the little bedroom had a door that opened on to a small private patio area. The patio was mainly cement with a small fringe of dirt around it where we thought we could plant some flowers. We did buy some rose bushes, added manure, and planted them. The only things we succeeded in growing were the biggest horseflies known to man.

Before leaving on our honeymoon we furnished the place quite nicely. Bobbie worked for AMC, a buying organization for department stores, so we were able to get furniture at a 50 percent discount. We decided to make the living room our bedroom as well so we bought a pullout sofa that served as our bed, probably the most important piece of furniture for newlyweds.

We left a twenty-dollar bill in the apartment before flying out to Saint Thomas. It was a good thing that we did. We took a cab from the airport after returning from Saint Thomas and when I paid the cab driver his fare, I had exactly eleven cents left in my pocket, not enough for a tip. I went into the apartment to get money for the driver's tip and what was left of that twenty dollars had to buy food until our next payday.

Poor Bobbie. She had a tough introduction to married life. Not only were we both working fulltime but I was going to law school four nights a week. Occasionally, she would meet me in Greenwich Village after my classes and we would have dinner at a cheap spaghetti joint that we both enjoyed. More often than not, however, I would come home exhausted and we would have a quick bite and while I studied, Bobbie would type my classroom notes.

I continued to work in the Spare Parts department at Curtiss-Wright and continued with my third year of law school in the evenings. Bobbie worked until her seventh month of pregnancy when her health required her to stop working and prepare for the birth of our first child, Ann which occurred on April 5th, 1958. We decided that the little bedroom would be an ideal place to put the infant. The room was only big enough to house a crib, changing table, and small dresser. What we did not realize was the room was somewhat drafty because of the door leading to the patio. When Ann was a few months old, we moved her and her furniture into our bedroom/living room, and started a search for a new apartment. One of the things that accelerated the search was an event that took place one weekend evening when Bobbie was preparing dinner for my dad and Ida. Bobbie opened the cabinet under the sink and a million roaches came swarming out. Bobbie shrieked and came running out of the kitchen. Ida ran into the kitchen to see what was happening, discovered the bugs, and proceeded to clean up the mess. Puerto Rico all over again. Our landlord refused to provide an exterminator, so Bobbie canvassed our fellow tenants, and got each of them to agree to pay fifty cents a month for this needed service. We still had roaches on occasion but never to the extent that we had them on that memorable evening.

My job was becoming increasingly routine and boring. It became apparent to me and to my fellow management trainees that the only path to success at Curtiss-Wright was to join the Management Club and play the game of corporate politics. This was something that I had decided early in my career that I would never do and never have.

One by one, my fellow trainees found better jobs and left Curtiss-Wright. Frank had already left for Aerojet. Boone moved to Los Angeles and took over one of his father-in-law's automobile dealerships. Rod went to work for Bendix. Stan moved to Rochester and went to work for Kodak, and so on.

Midway through my fourth and last year of law school, we found a wonderful apartment located on the tenth floor of a building at 215 West 88th Street. It was a huge, rent-controlled apartment that had three bedrooms, a formal dining room, large living room, a kitchen with what was called a butler's pantry, and three bathrooms. It was over 2,000 square feet, and because it was rent controlled, we only paid $165.00 per month; that included all utilities.

Around the same time that we moved into our new apartment, my father offered me a job. He had invented the "hidden" zipper. This was a zipper that could be sewn directly into the seam of a garment with no placket necessary. Sleek and smooth, clothing designers loved it. He wanted me to be president of his company since he had several tax liens against him and needed to hide behind someone. Who better than his son? Bobbie and I loved my father dearly, but we had strong reservations about me working for him. Those fears later proved to be well founded. At any rate, his strong salesmanship and a raise of $50.00 a week more than I was making at Curtiss-Wright persuaded me to accept his offer.

After he taught me all aspects of the zipper business, I really started to like my job. I had more responsibility than at any time since I was in the military. Although I had the title of president, there was no question who the real boss was. One of my yearly assignments was to establish a distribution organization. I flew out to California to meet with a number of jobbers and distributors. I was very successful in that I signed up a number of them to carry our "hidden" zipper as part of their line of merchandise. I also had the opportunity to take Bobbie with me. We arranged to have Florrie take care of our daughter so we knew she was in capable hands.

We stayed at the Ambassador Hotel in Los Angeles, and while I was making my sales calls, Bobbie had the opportunity to do some sightseeing. I learned on that trip that, unlike in New York City, it was impossible to see anyone on Friday; that was a day reserved for golf. Boone Gross, one of my ex-trainees invited us to a memorable dinner at his house in Bel Air. Bel Air is a very exclusive part of L.A. where only the rich can live. Boone had married Sally Tuttle, the daughter of Holmes Tuttle, one of the biggest automobile dealers in the area and a member of the consortium that later managed to get Ronald Regan elected to the Presidency. Boone was no slouch himself. He had gone to Yale University and was the son of the President of the Gillette Razor Company. Sally prepared a terrific dinner, the main course being beef stroganoff. After we got back to the hotel, both Bobbie and I got sick as hell but we never let the Gross's know that they had almost poisoned us.

I had a follow-up trip to the West Coast about a month later. Bobbie could not go on this trip because Ann was being fretful and needed her mother. I decided to stop over in Las Vegas before proceeding to Los Angeles. I stayed at the Flamingo Hotel and had my first taste of gambling, Nevada style. While in the service, I had mainly played poker but there was an occasional Blackjack game so I knew the rules. After dinner, I went to the casino and sat down at a blackjack table and started to bet one dollar at a time. About midnight, I was ahead about $50.00 when a new dealer came to the table. The dealer was Milton Berle, the comedian, who was entertaining at the hotel.

"Come on kid, put up more than one dollar a bet."

"Sorry, Uncle Milty (which is what he was called on TV). That's all I can afford."

"Look kid, put up $5.00 a hand and I'll make you a rich man."

"OK, Uncle Milty, but you better be good to me!"

Well, Uncle Milty was throwing money at the table. He would hit a twenty and break or he would stand on eleven and everyone at the table would have a winning hand. He left the table after about a half hour and I was $500.00 ahead of the game. I thought I had found a new career, but at the end of the evening, or should I say morning, I had lost the $500.00 plus my initial stake. Oh well, on to Los Angeles.

These trips, although successful, caused me to miss quite a few law school classes. Luckily, my final year's courses were pretty easy and attendance was never mandatory. Ann was an infant then, and she was only 14 months old when I graduated in 1959. Naturally, as an infant, she did her fair share of crying when I got home from school, which made studying quite a challenge.

An incident occurred during my final year of law school, which, if I had ever considered the practice of law, cured me of that thought forever. My good friend, Dick Kessler, invited Bobbie and me for a night out on the town with him and his girlfriend, Gunilla (Ginny). Ginny was a gorgeous girl and one of the country's top fashion models. Dick got us a ringside table at the Copacabana, one of New York City's top nightclubs. We had a couple of cocktails, and the featured performer, Nat King Cole, was introduced and started to sing. Bobbie was humming along with him, not realizing that she could be heard. (How loud can one hum?) One of the waiters came over and asked her to stop, which she immediately did.

The next thing that happened was that a couple of waiters came over to our table and removed all of our drinks. Dick told the waiters to put the drinks back on the table right now and with that those goons grabbed Bobbie, Dick, and me and proceeded to shove us to a stairwell that led out to the street. Ginny, I think, must have slid under the table to hide. Once in the stairwell, these goons beat the crap out of us as they were shoving us up the stairs and out on to the street. They managed to break Dick's nose, gave me several bruises, broke my glasses, and twisted several fingers on Bobbie's hand. We wound up on the street and fortunately, I thought, there were several police officers present.

"Officer," I said. "I want to make a citizen's arrest of these so-called waiters who assaulted us in the club."

"Shut the fuck up and the three of you get in the patrol car right now!"

"I'm a law student and I know my rights and I want you to arrest these people for assault and battery, right now!"

"I'm arresting you three for being drunk and disorderly and taking you to the precinct headquarters. If you do not get into the patrol car this minute, I'll ram this night stick so far up your ass, it will come out your nose!"

Once at the precinct I thought I would have a better chance dealing with the officer in charge. Was I ever wrong!

"Sergeant, as a law student, I know what my rights are and I want you to make a citizen's arrest of those goons who pass themselves off as waiters at the Copacabana."

"Sonny, you better learn to keep your trap shut or I'll see to it that it's shut permanently, if you get my drift. Now I want the three of you to sit quietly in that cell over there until I can arrange to have a wagon take your sorry asses down to the tombs where you will spend the night before your arraignment tomorrow for being drunk and disorderly. One peep out of any of the three of you is going to have ugly consequences. Got that?"

Well, it didn't take long for the Paddy wagon to arrive and drive us to the tombs. Before I was placed in my cell for the evening, I was allowed to make one phone call. I called my father who arranged to have a lawyer bail Bobbie and me out of jail in the morning. Dick called his dad and made similar arrangements. The three of us were separated. They took Dick to the infirmary where he was treated for his broken nose. Bobbie went to a cell that housed several prostitutes who nicknamed Bobbie Sabrina, after a character in a movie by that name. Her cell was overcrowded, so she and the prostitutes took turns sitting on the lone cot. Not wanting to sit on the dirty floor, she stood most of the night. Before being escorted to my cell, I gave the guard some money and cigarettes to give Bobbie to tide her through the long night. She never got them but the prostitutes were kind and shared their smokes with her.

Spending a night in a jail cell was extremely frightening for all of us. It's hard to explain how you feel when they close the door on you and you cannot leave for any reason. Bobbie, being claustrophobic, suffered the most although I certainly felt trapped. The worst part of all was knowing that we hadn't done anything wrong and the bad guys were off scot-free. I planned all night to do something about that.

Morning finally arrived, and Archie Palmer, a flamboyant, theatrical lawyer came and made arrangements to get Bobbie and me out on bail. Archie was famous for his defense of Judith Copeland, a notorious Communist. Dick's father hired an ex-prosecutor to get Dick out of jail.

One of the first things I did when I was released from jail was to schedule an appointment with Professor McKenna, who taught the class in Criminal Law that I had taken the preceding year.

"Professor McKenna, why is it that when all the elements necessary to effect a citizen's arrest were present, the cops refused to do so?"

"John, what I teach in the Criminal Law classes is theory. What you experienced, unfortunately, is the practical application of law by the so-called local law enforcement personnel"

"Is what you're telling me, that although our rights were abused, we have no remedy in law?"

"No, that's not what I'm telling you. You can sue them civilly or you can bring criminal charges against them for assault and battery. However, I don't recommend that course of action for you and your friend."

"Why is that? We were damaged and unlawfully arrested and we are not supposed to do anything about it?"

"Remember, John, I told you there was a difference between the theoretical application of the law and the realistic application. You are going up against some very bad people. It is common knowledge that the Mafia controls the Copacabana and the cops in their precinct are on their payroll. I recommend that you leave it alone and I'm sure that if you don't cause them any grief, they will drop the drunk and disorderly charges against you, your wife, and your friend."

"Thanks, Professor. I appreciate your advice, but I have to do something to get even with those bastards."

Dick and I got together and decided to take some action. Despite the advice from our attorneys and my law school professor we instituted a lawsuit against the Copacabana for assault and battery and unlawful arrest. That was a sorry mistake. Not too many days after filing our lawsuit, while I was at work, my wife got an unbelievable phone call from Archie Palmer. Archie said that he had an anonymous phone call from a man who said, "If Mrs. Silberman wants to keep her baby, Ann, she'd better not ever let go of her hand when she walks past..." He then proceeded to list all the places Bobbie would take the baby for her walk, and hung up.

A little later, Archie received another call from someone who represented himself as a member of Carmine Desapio's staff. Desapio was head of Tammany Hall and had a reputation as an unscrupulous politician. The purpose of the call was to convince Archie that it was not in his best interest to represent the Silbermans in this matter.

After conferring with Dick, we all decided it was not wise to get killed by the Mafia for standing up for our rights. We instructed our attorneys to see if the Copacabana would drop the drunk and disorderly charges against us if we would drop our charges. They agreed to do so, in part, because Bobbie was visibly pregnant with Tracy and it would not be good PR to take her to court.

We later learned that Bobbie and I had technically not been arrested at all! There were no blotter entries in our names, neither at the precinct where we were first taken nor at the Tombs. Furthermore, when the arresting officer learned that Bobbie was pregnant, he offered to change his story to say that she had not been drunk and disorderly. What kind of games were they playing?

To this date, none of us know the reason why this situation took place. Bobbie and I speculated that perhaps Ginny was dating one of the Mafia guys who wanted Dick out of the picture. We thought this because Ginny was the only one who was not roughed up and came out of the incident unscathed. Dick, who later married Ginny, denies that possibility so I guess we will never know what really caused our misfortune. But we learned a valuable lesson. The good guys don't always win!

I graduated from law school in June of 1959. Luckily, the GI Bill of Rights paid for all my tuition, books, and gave me a small monthly stipend for living expenses. Graduating from law school really doesn't mean much unless you pass the bar exam. I took a bar review course that held classes every night, and weekends as well. I managed to find lots of excuses not to attend these classes, as I was really sick of the whole deal. After a couple of months, it was time to take the exam, which was given over two days. The exam consisted of a multiple-choice section and an essay section. In the essay section, a case was given and you had to figure out the applicable principles of law and apply them to the facts presented. This was an intense experience, but I thought I had done pretty well.

Several months after taking the exam, the results were mailed. I had passed the multiple-part section, but had failed the essay section; that meant I had failed the bar exam. I had a hard time dealing with this, so Bobbie and I drove up to Albany, New York, where the results of the exam were stored. We compared my answers to the model answers and we knew that my answers were right on. My damn handwriting did me in again as I am sure whoever graded my answers could not read them. I asked the person in charge if I could challenge the grading of my exam. He said I had the right to do so but in more than fifty years, nobody had successfully reversed the grade given. I got the message and since I had already decided the practice of law was not for me, I did not try again to pass the damn thing. Spending those four long years going to law school was not a total waste of time. The degree looked impressive on my resume and the knowledge gained has been helpful during my entire business life.

I started to assume more responsibilities in my father's zipper business. One of the components of a zipper is the slider. This is the little device that runs up and down the zipper opening it or closing it. Since our product was unique, the "hidden" zipper, we could not use a standard slider. My father invented a slider that would work with the "hidden" zipper. The problem was that it consisted of quite a few components that had to be hand assembled and that was costly. We decided that I should go to Japan and make arrangements to have the slider assembled there. The reasoning was that labor there at that time cost ten cents an hour and despite having to pay duty on the sliders, it was still much cheaper to have them made in Japan and shipped to our factory in New York.

I spent three weeks in Osaka, Japan, working with Japanese engineers. We put an organization together that was successful in assembling our sliders. Bobbie could not come with me on this trip because she was pregnant with Tracy and her doctor would not permit her to fly. I flew from New York City to Los Angeles. The plane was scheduled to have a one-hour layover in L.A. before proceeding to

Hawaii, and then on to Japan. When we landed in L.A. we were told that there were some mechanical problems and it would be several hours before we could leave.

I called my friend Boone who suggested that I grab a cab and come over to his house to kill some time. I had about five hours before the plane was to depart and Boone and I got thoroughly plastered while swapping stories about our Curtis-Wright days. I remember Boone poring me into a cab with a full glass of Scotch in my hand for the return trip to the airport. I have no idea how I got back on the plane but I do remember taking a seat in first-class although I only had a ticket for coach. I promptly fell asleep and I guess the stewardesses decided it was better to leave me alone rather than wake me up and have me go to my assigned seat. I was supposed to meet Bobbie's friend, Ginny at the Hawaii airport but I never did. I slept all the way to Japan.

My stay in Japan was memorable for many reasons. I found out that I could work with engineers, Japanese ones, no less, and have them develop a product that we needed. I had hired a translator who was also an engineer and that helped. On the last weekend, before heading home, my Japanese hosts arranged a surprise party for me. They took me to one of the most famous Geisha houses in Osaka. I had been under the impression that a Geisha house was just a fancy name for a whorehouse. Was I ever wrong! It is a place where Japanese businessmen go to entertain clients and associates. The girls that work there are extremely skilled entertainers and servers. During dinner I had two Geishas serving me, one on each side of me. They would cut up my food and feed me with chopsticks and make sure that my sake cup was always full. During and after dinner they played music on exotic instruments, and sang and danced. The dinner went on for hours, and I drank so much sake that I decided that it was okay for me to get up and dance with them. Evidently this was a no-no, but I was forgiven because I was a stupid American who didn't know how to behave as a proper Japanese gentleman would. At any rate, it was a first-class experience and my hosts made sure I got back to my hotel safely.

My father gradually gave me more and more responsibility until I was finally in charge of the entire business. What my father did was to concentrate on making deals. The biggest deal that he made turned out to be the undoing of both of us. He managed to merge us into a public corporation that was listed on the over-the-counter market. While I was proud of being the president of a public corporation at a young age, I now had to report to a board of directors that we did not control. After several months, it became apparent that the majority shareholders, who were Europeans, wanted the Silbermans out, so they could put their own people in charge and move the business to Germany. They succeeded.

My dad wasn't overly concerned because he was involved with many other ventures. I wasn't worried either. As president of a public company, I had many high-level contacts that I used to deal with on a daily basis. What a rude awakening I was in for. Now that I was unemployed, these same people that I did business with on a regular basis did not even bother to return my phone calls.

It didn't take Bobbie and me long to run through the meager savings that we had accumulated. We had two babies to feed and we were starting to feel desperate. In order to be able to look for a job in the day, I went to work selling *Life* magazines by telephone at night and on weekends. Bobbie began selling Avon products and between the two of us we had just enough money to put food on the table and pay the rent.

After several months my old friend, Frank Cleary, from the Curtiss-Wright days, wrote me and offered me a job at Aerojet General in Sacramento, California. He told me that I would be on the general manager's staff with a starting salary of $900.00 per month. Meanwhile, I had applied for and was interviewed for a top position at the Tidy Didy Diaper Company. The diaper company was privately owned and they wanted to bring in fresh management to run the company for the owners. Their plan was to hire me as the general manager but nobody in the company would know this but the owners. I would be required to learn the business from the ground up starting off as a driver of the truck that would pick up the shitty diapers and deliver fresh ones. I thought this was quite ironical because I had told Bobbie before we got married that if we had children, I would not change their diapers, and I never did.

We did not know how long it would take for the owners of the Tidy Didy Diaper Company to make a decision, so we accepted the offer from Aerojet General and started to make plans for our trip across the country. Since I had fallen in love with California when I was in the service, it was not too difficult a decision for me to make. What was difficult was the realization that we would be leaving family and friends behind but I needed a job and that was the paramount consideration. What helped, somewhat, was that Nina, Bobbie's mother, whom I dearly loved, decided to retire from her job, join us on our journey and live with us in Sacramento.

Chapter Six
Sacramento, California and Aerojet General Corporation

1961 - 1968

The Personnel Department of Aerojet sent me an official letter notifying me of my acceptance for employment with a specific start date. They also advised me that they would reimburse me for all expenses related to my move from New York City to Sacramento, California and that I should keep good records. They also sent me copies of the Sacramento Bee, the local newspaper, so I could get a feel for what the housing market was like.

Since Bobbie and I had always lived in apartments, we were a little perplexed at ads for homes featuring such things as built-ins and swamp coolers. We assumed that "built-ins" were bookcases and "swamp coolers" were places to store your beer. At any rate, we were delighted that we could rent an entire house containing these impressive features for as little as $135.00 a month.

We visited all of our friends and relatives to say our goodbyes. We had all of our stuff packed in boxes ready for the movers when I got a call from Aerojet telling me that my offer of employment was contingent on a security clearance that had not come through yet. They told me not to worry as this was just a formality and would only delay things by a few days. We sat on the boxes, had another round of drinks and "goodbyes", and when we finally got the word that we could leave, our relatives and friends breathed a collective sigh of relief that the "goodbyes" were finally over.

We had decided that we would drive across the country and arranged to have our little dog, Schatzie, flown to Sacramento. To this end, I swapped cars with my brother trading him my beloved Studebaker for his four-door Ford which was much more suitable for the transportation of three adults and two kids. Since we were broke, I borrowed money from my mother to put new tires on the car and pay for food and lodging during our trip. I repaid her when I got reimbursed from Aerojet.

Because I had to keep detailed records of our trip in order to get reimbursement from Aerojet, I saved our trip expense log. I look back in amazement as to how cheap it was to feed, lodge, and transport three adults and two children across the country back in 1961. We started our journey on April 18, 1961. Ann had just turned three years old and Tracy was an eight-month old infant. The first day we just wanted to get out of New York City so we only drove 30 miles and spent the evening in a motel in Woodbridge, New Jersey. Our dinner that night for the five of us cost $9.45 and our two rooms cost a total $23.00

The next day we decided to put some miles behind us so we drove 462 miles and stayed over in Warren, Ohio. Our breakfast cost $3.70, lunch was $3.50, and dinner was $12.20. The motel rooms that night cost us $14.40.

Driving many miles with two small children was quite a challenge. Tracy would spend a lot of time sleeping, but Ann had to be amused, and thank God we had Nina to play with her. After we stopped for gas or to go to the bathroom, Bobbie would walk down the road with Ann as far as she could until I caught up with her in the car. This little exercise seemed to satisfy Ann, and she would be content for the next couple of hours. Because Tracy was too young to walk, she was car-bound all day. When we'd get to our motel room, she would spend an hour creeping around and around the room as fast as she could and would try to climb up on the bed. She was exercising herself.

Dinner that night in Warren, Ohio, turned out to be quite an experience. Bobbie put Tracy in the highchair that the restaurant provided. Our waitress, trying to be helpful, slipped the tray onto the arms of the highchair but unfortunately caught Tracy's finger in the process. Tracy started to scream and no matter how much we tried to comfort her she wouldn't stop crying. Bobbie, in consideration of the other patrons in the restaurant, took the screaming infant into the ladies room. Nina and I immediately ordered martinis for us and had one sent into the bathroom for Bobbie. The waitress decided to set up a table in the lounge part of the bathroom so Bobbie could have her meal there while attempting to calm Tracy. Nina and I got a good laugh out of watching several women going into the bathroom, ostensibly to take care of business. They would come out seconds later with a puzzled expression, never having seen a woman and child eating dinner in a restroom. We couldn't imagine what they must have been thinking, but I'm sure they were strange thoughts. Bobbie said they would enter, see her there, wash their hands, and leave. No one used the facilities while she was there for those twenty minutes or so, but there was a mad dash when she returned to our table with the now mollified baby.

Our stops for the next two evening were Hillside, Illinois, and Carroll, Nebraska. We had now traveled 914 miles, or about one-third of the way to California. Somewhere between those two cities, I called my mother to see if there were any messages for me. There was indeed a message from the president of the Tidy Didy Diaper Company. I returned his call and he congratulated me and offered me the job as general manager of his company. Although I was sorely tempted to accept his offer, we were too excited about the prospect of living and working in sunny California. I thanked him for his offer and wished him well in finding a suitable replacement for me. On to North Platte, Nebraska.

We arrived in North Platte and found a lovely motel where we arranged for two rooms for a total of $13.00 for both. After dinner (cost $7.65), Bobbie and I wanted a night out on the town and Nina agreed to baby-sit the kids while we went out looking for fun. Our first stop was at a cocktail lounge near our motel. We chatted with a fellow that owned the local Ford Dealership and he told us that there was a great place nearby that had terrific music and dancing. We decided to go, and had our first taste of nightlife in the wild west. The music was all country and western which we had had very little exposure to in New York City. Each song contained a little story, mostly sad, about someone leaving someone or someone dying of a broken heart. The dancers were something straight out of a western movie. The guys all wore cowboy hats, boots, and jeans and the girls all had little cowgirl outfits. The dancing, as far as we could tell, consisted of stomping as loud as possible to the music. Fortunately, I was not dressed in my usual New York business suit mode. I had a leather jacket and slacks that, although not totally appropriate, were not as bad as a three-piece suit would have been. Bobbie looked great, as always, in whatever dress she had selected for our night out. After a few drinks, we got into the swing of things, and discovered that we could stomp with the best of them. We had a great time that night and it was nice to have a little time to ourselves, away from the kids and Nina.

Our next two stops were in Rawlins, Wyoming, and Salt Lake City, Utah. Our motel bill for two rooms in Rawlins was $13.50 and $14.00 in Salt Lake City. Our next destination was Winnemucca, Nevada where we again persuaded Nina to baby-sit the kids so that Bobbie and I could go to one of the local casinos for a night of gambling. This was her first exposure to Nevada style gaming. I, being the seasoned Las Vegas gambler, explained the rules of Blackjack to her and we started to play. We each had a stake of $20.00 that we could ill afford to lose; however, we needed some entertainment and there was nothing else to do. I, the big expert, managed to lose my $20.00 rather quickly. Bobbie, with beginners luck, or the luck of the Irish, or whatever, won over $90.00. We considered it a very successful evening and had a fun time.

Earlier that same day, we had stopped for lunch at a restaurant in Lovelock, Nevada. When we left, Bobbie forgot to take her jacket with her. When we discovered the jacket was missing, we called from a pay phone, and the manager of the restaurant said that she would ask one of the truck drivers to drop it off at our motel in Winnemucca. We thought to ourselves that we could kiss that jacket goodbye but it was indeed delivered to us with the ten-dollar bill that Bobbie had left in her jacket pocket still there.

The next and final stop before arriving in Sacramento was Sparks, Nevada. Here, we had to pay the outrageous price of $17.85 for our two motel rooms. Bobbie and I decided to try our luck in Reno, but there was no possibility of having Nina baby-sit again. She needed a night out, away from the kids, so the three of us drove to Reno together. We hired a motel maid to watch over the kids, something that would be unthinkable in today's environment.

We went to the famous Harold's Club for dinner and a night of gaming. At dinner, I explained the Blackjack rules to Nina, who, being a good card player caught on quickly. The three of us sat at the same table, and after playing for several hours, Nina leaned over and whispered in my ear.

"John, I have to go to the bathroom real bad, but I don't want to give up my seat at this table."

"Nina," I whispered back. "Leave your money on the table, and the dealer will hold your seat for you while you are away." With that, Bobbie and Nina left the table, went to the bathroom, came back, and we played for several more hours. I believe that Nina was having so much fun that she would have stayed at the table and suffered whatever the consequences were if I had not explained to her that it was OK to take a bathroom break.

The next morning we began the last leg of our trip, a short three-hour ride from Reno to Sacramento. On our way there, we drove through a tiny town by the name of Carson City, the capital of Nevada. Little did we realize that some thirty-seven years later, Carson City would become home to us. Our destination was the KoKoMo Motel in Rancho Cordova, then a suburb of Sacramento, now a city of its own. We arrived there on April 28, 1961, ten days after leaving New York City. We had traveled 3,053 miles, spent $24.40 for breakfasts, $26.95 for lunches, $84.35 for dinners, $152.75 for lodging, and $63.50

for gasoline.

Once at the motel, Bobbie and Nina couldn't wait to go look and see what they could find in the way of rental housing so I stayed and baby-sat the kids. After several hours, they returned to the motel, Bobbie in tears.

"Dear, please let's go back home. These little houses we saw are awful. For $135.00 you get rooms so small that our furniture will never fit. And do you know what a swamp cooler is? It's something that sits on your roof and spits out damp air into your house, definitely not air-conditioning."

"There's no going home, Bobbie. Our apartment has been rented and I don't have a job back there. We just got here and Monday we'll get a real estate agent and start all over. Now put on your bathing suit and we'll take the kids for a swim in the pool."

The next day, Frank Cleary came over to our motel to see how we were getting along. Frank knew my mother-in-law from the Greenwood Lake days but he had never met my kids. He was in for an interesting surprise. When he came into our room he also let in a large horsefly. Ann, having lived on the 10th floor of an apartment house in Manhattan, had never encountered such a dangerous insect, and became hysterical. Frank, not being used to children, cut his visit short and suggested that Bobbie and I come over to his apartment for a drink and have Nina take care of the children. Frank remained a bachelor until his dying day and I wonder if Ann's encounter with the fly had anything to do with it.

On May 1, 1961, I reported in for work at Aerojet General Corporation. It was my turn to be disillusioned. Frank Cleary met me at the gate and escorted me to Security where I had my picture taken for my badge. Next he introduced me to Don King, the Division Head and Jim Dannick, the department head. Frank was a supervisor and was my boss for a few months till he transferred to corporate headquarters in Southern California. Next, he took me to a six-man cubicle, where I was assigned a desk.

"Frank, you haven't introduced me to my secretary yet, and where is my office?"

"John, you don't get a private office until you become a supervisor and only department heads and above have secretaries."

"Christ, Frank, in New York I had a huge private office and my secretary had a secretary. What gives?"

"You'll find out soon enough and in the meanwhile here are some procedure manuals that you need to read."

Bobbie, who needed the car to search for a place to live, picked me up after work and it was my turn to cry. I couldn't believe that I was being paid $900.00 a month and had none of the perks that a salary like that should command. The reason for this became apparent to me in a little while.

In the meantime, Bobbie and Nina found a cute little house located at 2664 El Segundo Drive in Rancho Cordova. We rented it for $145.00 a month from Bart Dolman, a major in the air force who was stationed at Mather Field. We had no idea that we would have to pay extra for water, garbage, and heating. That made the house more expensive than our beautiful apartment in New York. The house had three tiny bedrooms, two baths, a kitchen and a large living room and separate family room. We used the family room as our dining room in order to accommodate our formal dining room set. The house also had an enclosed patio room overlooking a beautiful garden. Between the living room and the family room, there was a freestanding fireplace that could also be used for barbequing. Our little girls loved to race around and around this fireplace until they would collapse in a fit of giggles.

After several weeks of doing nothing at work except for reading the procedures manuals, I begged Frank to give me a meaningful assignment. He assigned me a project, all right! I was asked to do an organizational study of the Minuteman Program. This was the organization that developed and manufactured the solid propellant for the Minuteman missile. I spent two months studying this organization, and I couldn't believe the inefficiencies that I uncovered. They had about twice as many engineers than were needed, and they had lots of redundancies in the organizational structure. I wrote a beautiful report outlining what needed to be done and I estimated that if they followed my plan there would be a huge cost savings for the program.

Aerojet was a lot like the army. There was a chain of command that you had to follow. Before I could present my findings to the manager of the Minuteman Program, I had to get approval from my management. I called a meeting of my supervisor, my department head, and my division head to show them what I had uncovered. I was expecting accolades for a job well done! What I got was a lecture on the nature of a cost plus operation. The higher the costs, the higher the profits and that's why they had two employees for each one needed. I was told to rewrite the report and extol the virtues of the Minuteman organization. Needing a job, I did what I was told and got a compliment from the manager of the Minuteman Program for a splendid report. I told Frank, "No more studies. Find something else for me to do."

We were slowly starting to settle into our new environment. On most days Bobbie would drive me and pick me up from work. We only had the one car and she would need it for shopping and to take the kids to the playground. I bought a lawn mower to cut the grass because I was not about to use scissors as I was made to do in the army. Bart Dolman would show up on the first of every month to collect the rent. I poured him a few drinks on his first visit and that became standard procedure during the rent collecting process. The first time he came, he inspected his beautiful garden and complained that we were not taking care of it properly. We had noticed that it wasn't as neat and spiffy as it had been when we moved in, but we didn't know why, or what to do about it. He told us that we needed to weed the flower-beds on a regular basis. Being sophisticated ex-New Yorkers, we did not know a weed from a hole in the ground. What we accomplished for Bart was to pull out his precious chives and special rose bushes that he had transplanted from his mother's garden in Illinois. He was not a happy camper the next time he came to collect the rent, but after an extra drink or two, all was forgiven.

On one Saturday, shortly after we arrived, I decided that I wanted to take Bobbie, Nina, and the kids to San Francisco and show them the places I had been while I was in the army. I picked the wrong day. The temperature hit 116 degrees and my non air-conditioned Ford decided that it had gone as far west as it would go. The car died in Davis, California; fortunately, near a service station. The mechanic at the station was able to get it started again, but he said the engine was shot and I probably needed a new car. We got back into the boiling hot car and decided to go back home and forget about San Francisco. Bobbie stripped Ann down to her panties and Tracy to her diaper. Because it was unbelievably hot, Bobbie and Nina also stripped down to their bra and panties. I imagine that if I had been stopped by the Highway Patrol, we would have been arrested for indecent exposure. At any rate, we made it back home and we all slept on the floor in the living room that night because this was the only room in the house that was air-conditioned.

About the same time that I asked Frank for a different assignment, he was promoted and transferred to corporate headquarters in southern California. Frank asked Jim, the department head, to promote me as his replacement. Jim acknowledged that I was well qualified for the job, but promoted Mike instead of me. His reasoning was that I was too new to Aerojet and Mike had been with the company for over a year. Mike assigned me the job of writing the financial S.P.I's (Standard Practice Instructions) for the Solid Rocket Plant. This assignment, although somewhat boring, enabled me to learn the intricacies of accounting and financial management of a defense contactor.

As time went by, Bobbie and I, and Nina and the kids, began to adjust to life in California. The weather took a little getting used to. There were no four distinct seasons as we had experienced on the East coast. The summers were incredibly hot with many, many days over 100 degrees. The fall and spring were beautiful but the winters were so foggy you often could not see across the street for days at a time. During one of these spells, I asked a newcomer how she liked Sacramento. "Oh!" she replied. "I think I would like it very much, if I could see it."

I got back into playing tennis with some of my associates after work and on weekends. Aerojet had a marvelous recreation center and while I was playing tennis with my buddies, Bobbie and Nina would watch over the kids as they swam or played with the other Aerojet children. After playing we would take the kids to the local Dairy Queen and buy them Dilly Bars for a treat.

Our fourth wedding anniversary was on May 30, just about a month after arriving in Sacramento. After dinner, Bobbie and I went up to Raleys, the local market, to look for some reading material for the evening.

"Dear," I said. "This is crazy. Here it is our anniversary and we are going to spend it reading books?"

"John, what else can we do? There are no bars or clubs nearby and I don't feel like getting dressed up to go downtown."

"Tell you what. I heard that Lake Tahoe is just about an hour's drive from here. They have some casinos up there and maybe we will be lucky on our anniversary."

"OK. Let's go home and kiss the kids good night and tell Nina where we're going."

It was nighttime when we drove up to Tahoe so we didn't realize how curvy the roads were. We arrived at Harvey's Wagon Wheel about nine that evening. Harvey's at that time was just a small casino that also had a coffee shop. Now, it's a huge two-building structure with rooms and all kinds of bars and restaurants in addition to a monster gaming area. Although it is still called Harvey's, it was purchased by Harrah's a few years ago. We played most of the night and did not do well. We decided to have breakfast in the coffee shop and had a full meal consisting of bacon and eggs, toast, and coffee, all for $1.99 each. I persuaded Bobbie to break into the house money so we could gamble a little longer. Well, this time we were lucky and got all of our money back, plus a few dollars.

We had one hell of a trip back home. We had been up all night long and in order to keep me awake, Bobbie would talk to me and ask me questions. It was daylight now, and the ride home was scary. The road was extremely curvy in spots and back then there were no guardrails over Echo Summit. Had we known the road was like that, we would never have driven up there at night. We got home all right, but Nina was upset with us for staying out all night.

My department hired a few new industrial engineers within a few months after I was hired. One of them, Jerry Cohen, was to become my business partner and has been and still is one of my best friends. He, like all the rest of us, came to work full of piss and vinegar, and was determined to make Aerojet a more efficient operation. There was an old saying at Aerojet. "After six months of trying to fix the problem, you become part of the problem." Jerry, bless his heart, tried his best in the beginning, but like my Minuteman debacle, he became frustrated and came to the realization that he really could not accomplish anything worthwhile.

Three of us from our department, Drex Cox, Jerry, and I would meet on a weekly basis and discuss various business opportunities that were available. This, we reasoned, would provide a challenge for us and a chance to remain in Sacramento if Aerojet went down the tubes, which we knew it would some day. One such opportunity that we explored was a McDonald's franchise, the second one planned for Sacramento. We rejected this opportunity because there was a requirement that we would have to go through the McDonald's Hamburger College. None of us, highly educated professionals, wanted to get our hands dirty flipping hamburgers. What a mistake! Drex eventually decided on a pizza parlor and opened one in Roseville, California, a suburb of Sacramento. Jerry and I selected a "One Hour Martinizing" franchise and opened our first dry cleaners in January of 1965 in West Sacramento.

Meanwhile, my situation at Aerojet changed drastically. Aerojet was given an opportunity to present a proposal to the Sacramento Board of Supervisors. This proposal was for the development of a management information system for the local War-on-Poverty Agency, the S.A.E.O.C. (Sacramento Area Economic Opportunity Council). Nobody at Aerojet wanted anything to do with this since the company was a defense contractor and not a social organization. Aerojet, the largest private employer in Sacramento, needed to respond so I was volunteered for the job. The Board of Supervisors selected my proposal from among several submitted and Aerojet was awarded the contract. Naturally, since I had written the winning proposal, I was made the project manager with the responsibility for developing the system.

I put a team of four people together, an accountant, a business analyst, a systems analyst and myself. After several months of working with Marion Woods (Woody) the Director of the S.A.E.O.C., we had a system in place. Bobby Kennedy, who was the US Attorney General and was in charge of the War-on-Poverty, stated that this system was the best one in the entire country.

As a reward for this effort and in recognition of my prowess as a proposal writer and project manager, I was transferred to the Computing Sciences Department, headed up by an egomaniac by the name of Aaron Cole. My prediction for Aerojet was beginning to come true. Business was on the decline and in order to maintain the staffing in the Computing Science Department, the decision was made to sell the excess capacity, both people and machine time to state and local government agencies.

Aaron rented an office in a downtown building for Pete Crockett and me. That way we would be close to Sacramento County and the state agencies that we were selling to. Pete and I were very successful and placed dozens of programmers and analysts with the various organizations that we serviced. I was also responsible for writing proposals to develop specific applications. One of my biggest achievements was writing a winning proposal to Sacramento County for the development of an automated child support system. This was the first system of its kind in the country. The system would produce automated "Warrants for Arrest" and automated "orders to show cause" as well as notifying the caseworkers when certain actions were required.

I bid this contact for a fixed price of $23,000.00. I was slightly off in my cost estimate. It cost Aerojet in excess of $500,000.00 to develop and implement the system on the County's computer. Naturally, Aerojet wanted to recover as much of this money as possible so I was tasked with the job of negotiating with the County. The fellow that I had to negotiate with was Tim Leslie, a budget analyst for

Sacramento County. I was pretty successful in recovering a portion of the development funds and Tim and I became friends and tennis buddies. Tim later on became a California Assemblyman and State Senator. In 1996 Tim made a run at becoming Lt. Governor. I had not seen Tim for many years but I contributed generously to his campaign. Bobbie and I were invited to a dinner fund raising affair for Tim. When he approached our table to shake hands he didn't have a clue as to who I was and didn't have any recollection of our past friendship. So much for politicians. He did not win the election, which pleased me.

I firmly believed that the child support system that we had developed had the potential for being the basis for a national marketing campaign. The marketplace was immense and ripe for a system like this. I, however, could not convince my management to give me the necessary funds to launch a national campaign. I was told that I could personally try to market the system but was not given any additional support. I did manage to sell a feasibility study for Los Angeles County but that was the end of it. Other companies stepped into the breach and literally made hundreds of millions of dollars selling and installing child support systems based on the concepts that I had created. Oh well!

Life was expanding on the home front. Our son Patrick (John Patrick) was born on June 24, 1963. Now we had three kids and three adults living in a relatively small house. We found a beautiful model home not far from where we were currently living. It had four bedrooms, two baths, a small, but extremely efficient kitchen, a formal living room, and a huge family room. The construction company was framing a house just like the model on a cul-de-sac located on Grinnell Way. The house was at the back end of the cul-de-sac and had a huge back yard suitable for a swimming pool.

The sales price for this house was $22,500.00. Because I did not have enough money for a normal down payment, I used my GI Bill and was able to purchase the house with nothing down and $99.00 for closing costs. Part of the process for purchasing the house was for the lender to examine my credit. Bobbie and I were in for a big shock. I had a tax lien against my name in the amount of $4,000.00 that had to be cleared before the sale could be executed. Seems that the New York City company that I had been president and director of did not pay employment taxes like they should have. My father had no official position in the company and all the other directors were in Europe, so I got stuck with the tax bill. I called my dad for help, but he was in one of his periodic down periods and did not have any cash to spare. We met with the IRS agent, a really nice fellow, and signed an agreement to pay the debt over two years. The lien was cleared and we took possession of our first house after it was completed, in about six month's time.

In order to help pay off this $4,000.00 debt, I got Bobbie a job as a secretary at Aerojet. We would drive to work together, meet at the end of the day, and drive home. Nina, meanwhile had moved back east to live with Fla so we had no one to take care of the children while we were both working. We solved that problem by hiring Genevieve, a French lady, who was the mother-in-law of one of the airmen stationed at Mather Field. She moved into the bedroom that Nina had. Not only did she take care of the children, she also cooked fantastic meals for the family. Bobbie worked for approximately one year at Aerojet before she had to quit because of the impending birth of Patrick. Because of this debt, I took a second job selling pots and pans at night. I was totally unsuccessful in this endeavor and went back to my old skill of selling *Time* magazine over the telephone at night and on weekends. After Patrick's birth we let Genevieve go and Nina decided to come live with us again after we moved into our new home.

Nina was suffering from Paget's disease, a sickness where the bones soften and recalcify in strange positions. As the disease progressed, Nina went from having to use a cane, to a walker, and finally to a wheelchair. We couldn't leave her alone with the children anymore and that kind of put a crimp on our evenings out except for visiting with the neighbors. She needed help going to the bathroom and that was not a problem during the day. We gave her a little bell, which she could ring when she needed assistance during the night.

She would not accept my assistance, so the burden fell on Bobbie. One time, about a year after she was confined to the wheelchair, she rang the bell nine times during the night, which exhausted Bobbie, who had to take care of three active children during the day.

Bobbie and I had a tearful discussion the next morning and came to the terrible conclusion that Nina would have to go into a nursing home. We called Fla to tell her about what we needed to do, and she insisted that we put Nina on a plane back to New York because she would not permit her mother to be sent to a nursing home. We put Nina on a plane a few days later, and within three weeks Fla put her in a nursing home back east. Fla just had no concept of how much help her mother required.

In mid 1964, Jerry Cohen and I decided to invest in a "One Hour Martiizing" franchise. The total investment including all the machinery, equipment, and installation was $50,000.00. Jerry and I each had to put up $4,000.00. As usual, I did not have any money, so I borrowed $1,000.00 each from Nina, my sister, my mother, and Fla.

In order to save some money, Jerry and I assisted in the installation of the equipment. One rainy day right before Thanksgiving, Jerry and I were on the roof of the building, trying to help with the placement of the huge "One Hour Martiizing" sign and giant clock which went on top of the sign. The sign was so heavy that it broke the boom on the truck that was lifting it. We had to stay on the roof while the driver went to find a truck with a more substantial boom. I went home that night soaking wet and wondering what the hell I had got myself into.

Our grand opening in January 1965 was also quite exciting. As we started the plant in operation, one of the valves on the cleaning machine was defective and let loose a flood of toxic solvent on the floor. All of us, the cleaner, the presser, the counter-girl, Bobbie, Jerry and I went racing out to the street so we could breathe. Bobbie ran next door to the bank to get help and within a few minutes the fire engines arrived and a fireman with a gas mask went into our plant and shut off the valve. What a great beginning! When trying to decide on a name for our corporation, we came up with Vayo Inc. which was kind of backwards for Oy Vay, and rightfully so.

After a few months of losing money, Jerry and I decided that we'd better learn something about the dry-cleaning business. There was a course in dry-cleaning given at Laney College in Oakland at night and Jerry and I both enrolled. We would drive 70 miles from Aerojet after work to attend the classes. We learned how to recognize stains and remove them with special spotting chemicals. We learned how to press all different types of garments. To complete the course, we had to take a final exam. This exam consisted of identifying and removing ten different stains, and pressing four garments. Jerry passed this exam on the first try, but it took me three tries before I passed. I received a certificate from the State of California recognizing me as a licensed dry-cleaner. I had the certificate framed and mounted it on the wall right next to my law school diploma.

After we learned something about the business, we changed our staff, hired more competent help, and started to become profitable. Jerry and I would take turns working on Saturdays and Bobbie worked there during the week. We didn't pay her a salary but we did pay her for the babysitter that she hired to look after our kids. One Saturday while I was working at the cleaners, a beautiful Cadillac pulled up to the front door and a nice looking gentleman came in carrying a vast quantity of women's clothing. The clothing was very fancy and consisted of evening dresses, nightgowns and mini skirts, etc. Because this was a big order, and in order to try and secure future business, I struck up a conversation with the gentleman. I said:

"That's a beautiful car you have out there and these are elegant garments."

"Well, that's very kind of you."

"I just opened this dry cleaning business a few months ago and I really appreciate your business. By the way, what business are you in?"

"Tomatoes," he replied. Because there was lots of farmland in the area, I believed this to be true.

On Monday morning, I had coffee with Jerry at Aerojet and told him about this rich guy who was in the tomato business. We agreed that if there was a business opportunity in growing tomatoes, we should look into it further. A few months later we found out this guy was in the tomatoes business, all right. He was the chief pimp of West Sacramento and ran a stable of whores in the many motels located in the community. Bobbie had the distinct pleasure of dry-cleaning the prostitutes clothing and Jerry and I had the distinct pleasure of feeling like fools. We knew the "tomatoes" business was profitable, but not for us.

One day a lady came into the shop to pick up a man's suit that she had left a few days before to be dry-cleaned. When I handed her the suit, she told me that it was not her husband's because it was the wrong color and size. When we researched the problem, we discovered that we had given her husband's suit to a different person. If that wasn't bad enough, the suit went to the local funeral parlor and had been used to clothe the corpse that had been buried that morning. We discussed exhuming the guy to get the suit back, but cooler heads prevailed and we told the lady with the missing suit to go buy her husband a new suit since we could not find his and it was probably stolen.

At Aerojet, I was getting more and more involved with the selling of computer systems, contract staff, and machine time. We sold mainly to the various California state agencies and the county of Sacramento. I was always pretty good as a salesman and I took to this type of sales with enthusiasm and much success. I convinced Aaron that we needed to expand this business into other marketplaces. I decided that the States of Nevada and Washington were likely candidates for our services. Since it was my idea, I was tagged with the responsibility of developing these markets. This was the beginning of what would become many years of traveling and being away from my family during the week.

I met Gordon Harding, the Director of Centralized Computing for the State of Nevada. Gordon and I hit it off, and I obtained many lucrative contracts for Aerojet. I was also successful in Olympia,

Washington and had a staff of Aerojet computer specialists working for the State Department of Institutions. Also a lucrative contract.

While I was out marketing Aerojet's computing capabilities, Jerry was busy expanding the Vayo Corporation. We opened a second dry-cleaners in Woodland, California. Jerry also began selling draperies that he arranged to have manufactured elsewhere. He sold to private homes as well as apartment complexes. Aerojet continued to suffer a serious decline in business and Jerry along with thousands of others was laid off in 1967. He began working full time in our business that by then had the capability of supporting him financially. As long as I continued to have success selling, I did not have to worry about being laid off.

Right before Christmas in 1967, Aaron sent me to Miami, Florida, where I was to write a proposal to the Board of Supervisors of Dade County for a computer system. I was not a happy camper being sent away from home before the holiday season, but I went anyway. I stayed in a hotel that advertised that it had stenographic services. In the normal course of writing a proposal, I interviewed the individual supervisors so I could determine the requirements for the system. At the end of the day, I would go back to my room and dictate my findings to the hotel stenographer that I had hired for that purpose. The stenographer was a little old lady, and I got a kick out of the fact that she made me keep the door open while I dictated my proposal to her.

I finished writing the proposal, priced it, and called back to Aaron for his approval before submitting it to the board. Aaron agreed with my pricing so I called the chairman of the board to select a date for a presentation before the full board. I also disclosed the price for the system to see if it was in the ballpark of what they expected, and it was.

Early the next morning, Aaron called me and told me I had to double the price for the system. I explained to him that I had already told the chairman what the price was but Aaron insisted that I do as I was told. It was too late to warn the chairman as I only had a few hours before I was to present the system to the Board. I presented the system and when it came time to disclose the price, I told them that I had erred in my calculations and that the price was double what they had expected. I flew home in time for Christmas determined never to be embarrassed like that again. I was going to quit my job at Aerojet. Naturally, the Board rejected Aerojet's proposal.

A few weeks later, in January of 1968, I requested a meeting with Aaron Cole. I explained to him that what he did to me in Florida was inexcusable, that my integrity had been violated, and I had no choice but to resign effective immediately. He accepted my resignation but told me that it was not because of the reasons I had given him. He said that if I would meet him for lunch the next day he would make everything clear to me. I agreed to the lunch, cleared out my desk, and left Aerojet for the last time, after having worked there for over seven years. I left with lots of memories and no regrets.

Chapter Seven
Boothe Resources International

1968 - 1971

I met with Aaron the following day for lunch.

"John," he said, "Although, it was my decision to send you to Florida right before Christmas, I was under a lot of pressure from one of Aerojet's directors to make sure we delivered a proposal to the Dade County Board of Supervisors, and I knew you would come through. When he read your proposal, he directed me to have you double the price because he thought he had the chairman in his pocket and that the increased cost would not matter."

You spineless prick, I thought. "Well that explains that," I said. "But you should have stood up to him and not have me make a fool of myself."

"John, that's not the reason I asked you to lunch and that's not the reason I accepted your resignation so readily. You know I have been trying to sell the senior management of Aerojet with the idea of setting up my organization as a separate company so that we could be more competitive in the market place. Because their main business is producing rocket engines, they'll let us play at marketing computer services but they will not endorse the concept of establishing a separate entity.

"I met with the people from Boothe Computer in San Francisco. That's the organization from which Aerojet leases their IBM computers. Boothe is a third-party leasing company and they want to establish a software subsidiary. They want me to be part of it so I submitted my resignation from Aerojet a few days before you did and I am in the process of planning for the new company. I'm sure I can offer you a job with a significant increase in salary, and I would like you to come to San Francisco with me and meet the key players. What do you say?"

"Well, since I'm out of work and have nothing better to do, I'll go but I'm not making you any promises."

A few days later Aaron and I drove into San Francisco and stayed at one of the fancy townhouses that the Boothe Computer Company owned. The next day we went to their offices, located in the Alcoa building. I met several of the Boothe executives, but I was more interested in meeting the people who had been selected to run the new company, Boothe Resources International.

I met them and I was blown away. Ron Morrison had been hired as president of the new company. If you were making a movie, and needed a president for central casting, Ron would have been your boy. He was tall, good-looking, had a commanding air about him, and was a former executive of IBM. Stu Arinoff, also an ex-IBM executive was administrative vice president of B.R.I. Pete Melitz and Aaron Cole, both named vice presidents, rounded out the executive staff for the fledgling company. Pete was in charge of Education and Training and Aaron was in charge of Computer Operations and Professional Services.

I had known Aaron for the better part of seven years, and did not care for the man. Like most insecure individuals, he had a brusque manner and a huge ego designed to hide his insufficiencies. What he was good at, however, was surrounding himself with capable people and permitting them to do their jobs. He was also a master at playing corporate politics, something I disliked and always refused to do.

After spending two days in San Francisco, and thoroughly enjoying the people I met, I was offered a job as Regional Manager of Professional Services. I decided to accept this offer for three reasons. One, the salary was very good. Secondly, the corporate office was going to be established in Los Angeles. That meant Aaron would have to move to L.A. and I would open an office in Sacramento for my operation. The third, and perhaps most significant factor in my reasoning was that I would be starting a business from scratch and I could mold it the way I wanted to. It was a challenge that had particular appeal to me, and one that I would experience several more times in my career.

Living in the cul-de-sac on Grinnell Way was a hoot. We had a huge back yard where we eventually put in a swimming pool and a beautiful rose garden. Our kids became strong swimmers and all of them won numerous ribbons in the various swim meets that they competed in. In the summertime, on weekends and evenings, our neighbors and their children would come over to our house for a swim, barbeque, and cocktails. We had great neighbors and formed lifetime friendships with many of them. They were from all walks of life, from a doctor, to a retired military officer, to a career state worker to several like me who were budding business executives and entrepreneurs. We had a marvelous social life and did not even have to leave the cul-de-sac to have lots of fun.

Bobbie never had a chance to go to college after she graduated from high school. Her dad died when she was an infant and her mother did not make enough money to send her to college even though she had been accepted at Cornell University. She had to work to support herself and to help Nina with the rent, etc. Now that the girls were in school full time, and Patrick was old enough to go to day care, Bobbie decided that she wanted a college education. At the age of 33, she enrolled at American River College, a local junior college. She went part-time, and as an excellent student, graduated with honors four years later. She then enrolled as an English major at the University of California in Davis.

When I accepted Aaron's offer to be the regional manager, I literally had to start from scratch. I opened an office in downtown Sacramento to be close to my government clients. I bought some second-hand office furniture, hired a secretary, and began raiding Aerojet's Computer Sciences Department. I hired a number of their senior computers specialists before I got a letter from Aerojet's lawyers telling me to cease and desist. Aaron proved to be clever in hiring me because the people that I hired would have never gone to work for him directly. He was not a popular manager at Aerojet and the programmers and analysts that I brought on board were all my friends and were willing to take a chance on me.

We started to crank out proposals to the same organizations that I had done business with previously, and within a few weeks the contracts started to roll in. I hired additional staff to fulfill these contracts and my little organization started to bring in some serious money.

Aaron invited me down to Los Angeles to inspect the corporate headquarters and the computer facilities that B.R.I. had opened. I was shocked at what I saw. The corporate offices were located on Wilshire Boulevard, in an expensive building. The data center was across the street, in an equally expensive building. When I visited the president's office, I couldn't believe my eyes. The office was huge and was decorated with expensive art works including a Persian rug. His office furniture was made from teak wood and must have cost a fortune. That boy sure could spend money!

The other offices were also furnished expensively but not to the extent that Ron Morison's was. I noticed a number of people in various offices who were busy writing away. I asked Aaron what that was all about. He told me that Pete Melitz had hired a staff of instructors who were busy writing lesson plans for courses that B.R.I. was going to teach. It amazed me that nobody thought it might be a good idea to try and sell some courses before investing in so many people.

When I went across the street to inspect the data center, I was in for more surprises. The company had invested in and installed an IBM 360-50 and an IBM 360-30. The theory was that B.R.I. would act as the data center for a number of companies in the Los Angeles area. It might have been wise to line up some companies before making this substantial investment in computer power. What was worse was that they had hired a number of programmers whose role would be to serve the companies who were using the data center. Again, this was a clear display of having the cart before the horse. It was apparent to me that these ex-IBM executives were used to spending lots of money and didn't have a clue as to how to manage a start-up business. Sort of like the dotcom bust of the late 90's. I went back to Sacramento, to my cheap office with second hand furniture, and started to generate more profits for these fools to spend.

About once a year, my mother would fly out to visit us for a week to ten days. After her first trip, we all dreaded her arrival and couldn't wait for her departure. The first time we took her out for dinner with the kids we learned that we should go early when there were few customers dining. The waitress took our drink order. My mother ordered a whiskey sour, Bobbie and I ordered Scotches, and the kids asked for cokes. The waitress brought us each two drinks.

"Why did you bring two drinks, when we only ordered one?" my mother asked.

"It's Gollywomper Hour," the waitress replied brightly, happy to be giving a bargain. "You get two drinks for the price of one." Indignantly, Mom replied, "If I wanted two drinks, I'd ask for two drinks. Now you take the extra drinks off the table right now!"

With that, the young waitress turned bright red, did as she was told, and we had a different waitress for the rest of the meal. The kids attempted to slide under the table but Bobbie and I caught them just in time. On another occasion she said in her usual loud strident voice, "Look at that poor man sitting over there. Isn't he the ugliest man you ever saw?"

The kids succeeded in crawling under the table this time. Fortunately, this turned out not to be so embarrassing after all, because the rather ordinary looking man turned his head to see who the "ugly" man was. Bobbie did a lot of special cooking during Mom's visits because we all hated the nasty situations she created in restaurants.

Another irritating aspect of her visits was the mandatory shopping. My mother was very generous in the gift-giving department but it was the manner in which she bestowed her largesse that was annoying. She would always ask us what we wanted but she had already made up her mind as to what she was going to buy. Then came the dreaded trip to the department store. On one visit, she decided that Bobbie needed a food processor, although Bobbie didn't want one. But it had to be a processor that could take a whole box of cake mix in one batch

We took her to Macy's and as fate would have it there was a woman, not a Macy's employee, demonstrating a certain brand of food processor. My mother was not familiar with this particular brand so she asked the demonstrator where the brand that she had heard of was located, and then she asked her if her processor could mix a cake in one batch. The woman said she didn't know where the other appliances were because she was not a salesclerk, only a demonstrator. And she didn't know the answer to the cake mix question because nobody had asked her that before. My mother turned to us and said in a voice loud enough for everybody to hear,

"See, son, you can't get decent help any more. All these stores do is hire *Schwartzas* (Yiddish for Black) and Puerto Ricans to be sales clerks and they don't know anything."

The fact that the demonstrator was a middle-aged white woman didn't seem to matter to dear old Mom. Bobbie came to the rescue, grabbed the processor that Mom was familiar with, and we hustled her to the purchase counter. Mom wasn't through embarrassing us yet. She insisted on speaking with the department manager to complain about the clerk who didn't know anything. The manager quickly realized what she was dealing with, and promised to take prompt action. There was more. When the clerk asked for her drivers license or some other form of identification to verify her out-of-state check, my mother replied that she didn't drive, and with that she opened her blouse, pointed to the scar where her pacemaker was located, and told the clerk that this was her only identification and that was all she was going to show. I wished that I had a camera to capture the look on that poor clerk's face. Somehow we managed to escape from Macy's before they called the Looney-bin police.

My mother's last visit to California occurred in 1977, when Jimmy Carter was the president. I would come home from work, dog-tired, having made some difficult business decisions. The moment I came through the door she would be in my face. This was the period in our country's history when President Carter had the horrible responsibility of having to deal with the Iran hostage crisis.

"Johnny, if you were the president, what would you do to free the hostages?"

"I'm not the president, Mom."

"Yes, but if you were the president, what would you do?"

"I don't know, Mom. I am not the president and I can't pretend that I am."

"This is a serious matter, John, and you must make a decision!"

"I have to make business decisions all day long and I don't have to make any decisions about our hostages!"

This conversation went on every day during her visit, kind of like the Chinese water torture, a drip at a time. On her last night during dinner she started up again and wouldn't let it drop. All the years of patiently listening to her bullshit, and responding politely, finally caught up with me. My fuse had burnt down. I told her "to shut the fuck up", turned red, grabbed for her cane, and was going to beat her to death right at my dining room table. Fortunately, Bobbie and the kids got hold of me before I could take the first swing. She fled the dining room, packed her bags and Patrick drove her to the airport. It was many years before I would speak to her again. But Bobbie kept in touch, calling her dutifully once a week. So even though I would not speak to her, Bobbie would tell me how she was doing.

My Sacramento office of B.R.I. really started to take off. I successfully persuaded one of the "big eight" (at that time) accounting firms to partner with me in the development of a new accounting system for Sacramento County. The manager of Peat-Marwick, Bruce Joplin, and I became close friends. After the system was successfully installed, Bruce quit Peat-Marwick, formed his own company, Sartoris, and had many profitable years installing this system in county governments all over the country. In the mid-eighties, Bruce cashed out by selling Sartoris to E.D.S.

I also enjoyed great success in developing and installing systems for the State Department Of Education. I was so successful, that I was able to induce Dr. Grossman, the manager of the Department of Education's Information Technology group to join B.R.I as manager of my Education Division. I was also able to hire Bob Hansen, an ex-IBM salesman to head-up my Transportation Division. Both of these individuals helped me expand the business into other marketplaces and I eventually opened offices in Olympia, Washington, Los Angeles, California, Springfield, Illinois, and New York City.

While I was expanding the consulting business around the country, big changes were occurring at corporate headquarters in L.A. The executives at Boothe computer got wise to Ron Morison's spending habits, fired him, and replaced him with Herb Blodget, one of the Boothe Computer executives. Pete Melitz and his entire staff were let go because they had failed to sell even one course. The Data Center started to acquire some customers so I was not the only one producing revenue for the company. In 1970, Aaron promoted me to Vice President of Professional Services, and strongly suggested that I move to corporate headquarters in L. A. because he needed my help.

Bobbie and I had lived in Sacramento for nine years and decided a change of scenery might be fun. So we decided to move after school was out. Bobbie had completed her junior year at the Davis Campus of the University of California and, with some difficulty, was able to transfer her credits to U.C.L.A. She graduated with a B.A. in English in 1971.

One of our neighbors, a real estate agent, helped us rent our lovely home on Grinnell Way to four fellows who worked for the sheriff's department. What a mistake! Four months after we moved to Los Angeles, Jackie Minners, our real estate agent, told us that we had to get rid of our tenants. They were bachelors who had wild parties unsuitable for a family neighborhood. I flew up to Sacramento to inspect my house and could hardly believe the mess that they had made. My swimming pool was full of algae despite the chemicals I had left and the instructions that I had given them for its maintenance. There were also hundreds of beer cans on the bottom of my pool. The inside of the house was also a mess with the smell of marijuana permeating the bedrooms.

Jackie was able to evict them, cleaned up the house and pool at a considerable cost to us, put it on the market for sale, and sold it within a few months. We hated to sell our first home but Los Angeles was too far away to be able to manage a rental.

When we first moved to L.A. Aaron tried to persuade us to rent a house in Sherman Oaks, where he lived. Knowing that I would be doing a lot of traveling around the country, Bobbie and I decided to find a place relatively close to the airport. As luck would have it, we found a terrific house on one of the few residential streets off Wilshire Boulevard. It was a huge two-story with a large swimming pool and cabana in the back. It was like living in a small town, but if you walked one block from our street, Warner Drive, you were right smack in the heart of a major metropolitan area with office buildings, department stores, and shops. Skinny-dipping in our pool was not an option because the windows of large office buildings had a clear view of our pool.

One of the benefits of living where we did was that I could get to the airport using the surface streets. I did not have to drive on the freeways that were always crowded. My job required extensive traveling and frequently I would leave home on Monday, travel to two or three different cities, and come home exhausted on Friday evening or Saturday morning. Both Aaron and Herb appreciated my efforts and the results that they achieved. Herb told me that he wasn't going to be the president of B.R.I. forever because he was needed back at Boothe Computer and that good things were in store for me.

Meanwhile, back in Sacramento, Jerry was expanding our business. We had purchased a commercial laundry, had two dry cleaning plants, and a separate facility for cleaning drapes. Jerry was also busy selling and installing drapes for both residential and commercial clients. He wanted me to return to Sacramento and help him run the business because it was too much work for just one person to handle. I wasn't quite ready as I was having too much fun building up my division; however, I was getting very tired of all the travel that was required of me.

One day towards the end of 1971, Aaron called me in Chicago where I was working with a client.

"John," he said. "I've got some very good news for you. I have been appointed President of B.R.I. and I want you to become my executive vice president."

Shit, I thought. *I've been carrying this son of a bitch for years now and he gets all the credit and I do all the work. After what Herb told me I thought that I was going to get the job but Aaron knew how to play the game.*

"Congratulations," is what I said. "I'll see you back in L.A. when I finish up with my client."

That evening I called Bobbie from my hotel room and told her what transpired. We both agreed that this was extremely unfair to me and since I had the option of returning to Sacramento to work with Jerry, I should quit B.R.I. and let Aaron swim by himself. When I got back to L.A. I submitted my resignation to Aaron who went into a state of shock, and took off for home and a several-day binge. I did not feel one bit sorry for him since he had a history of using people and taking all the glory for himself.

Within a year, there was nothing left of B.R.I. Dr. Grossman formed a company with what was left of my Education division and Bob Hanson and Neal Jones formed Hansen and Associates and took over my transportation division. All the good people that I had recruited left for other jobs where they enjoyed much success. None of this would have been necessary if only Boothe Computer had the foresight to appoint me president. Unfortunately, I would not play the game of corporate politics then and never.

Chapter Eight
Vayo Inc.

1971 - 1980

Bobbie and I decided that we wanted to live in pretty much the same area of Sacramento that we did before we moved to L.A. The kids liked that idea too because they had really missed their friends from Grinnell Way. We made a trip to Sacramento and found a two-story model home that we really liked. We arranged to have the house built on a vacant lot on Great Falls Way, directly across from an open field, that was zoned for a church site. The only problem was that it was going to take six months to build our house, so we had to find an interim house to live in, which we did. Because I had to pay for the move back to Sacramento, we got rid of thousands of pounds of crap that we had accumulated over the years. We still had 10,000 lbs. to move so it was a fairly costly experience, especially since we had to move again in six months.

I started to work with Jerry in our business. Although our corporate name was Vayo, we did business as Fabricare. Jerry was very successful in selling drapes for use in office buildings, apartment houses, and private residences. I tried my hand at this part of the business and we would have gone down the tubes, if it were up to me. I did not have the patience to sit down with some housewife, show her fabric samples, measure her windows, and wait for her to decide what she wanted. Selling a couple of hundred dollars worth of draperies was a far cry from selling million-dollar computer systems.

Jerry had the drapes that he sold manufactured at several different facilities. Since we did not have control of this process, there were frequent quality and delivery issues. We decided that our clients would be better served, if we had our own manufacturing facility. The first step in this process was to get an S.B.A. (Small Business Administration) loan. In order to obtain this kind of loan, we first had to be refused by a commercial bank. That part was easy. We tried several banks, including our own, Wells Fargo, and they were all delighted to turn down our loan application. Getting an S.B.A. loan was a long, tortuous, bureaucratic process, but we finally got $50,000.00 which was the amount needed in order to establish our own drapery manufacturing facility. Years later, we tried for another loan from the S.B.A but were turned down because we had paid off the first loan. We were actually told by some government official that if we had been in default of the first loan, we would be eligible for further loans. Go figure.

We set up our manufacturing facility at Del Monte Street in West Sacramento. We also moved our drapery cleaning operation to the same location. These two parts of our business worked hand in hand. Frequently, the apartment house drapes would fall apart in the cleaning process because of sun damage. That triggered Jerry into making a call on the apartment house where he would sell replacement drapes for the ones that were ruined. One of my responsibilities was to call on the apartment house managers and sell them on why Fabricare was the best drapery cleaner in town and secure their business. Again, not the challenge of marketing computer systems, but it was necessary.

We placed Fabricare on the State's bidder's list for cleaning and making drapes. One of the biggest awards that we received was to make replacement drapes for the ten-story Water Resources Building in downtown Sacramento. Since the State awarded contracts based on the lowest price, it soon became apparent why we were so lucky. We had neglected to include the cost of taking down and reinstalling the drapes in our bid. This piece of stupidity gave me and my son,

Patrick, and Jerry and his son, Steve, plenty to do in the evenings and on weekends. I remember standing on a desk in one of the manager's offices, hanging drapes. Two years previously, I had made a presentation to that manager and his staff for the acquisition of a major computer system that they subsequently purchased. One of life's funny twists!

Shortly after we moved back to Sacramento from L.A., one of my ex-managers from the B.R.I. days, Jack Watts, invited Bobbie and me to attend a San Francisco 49ers game. This was the first professional football game that we ever saw, and what a game it was! San Francisco was playing the Dallas Cowboys for the Divisional Championship. The Niners were way ahead with only a few minutes to go when Roger Staubach, the Dallas quarterback, engineered a magnificent comeback and won the game for the Cowboys with less than two minutes to go. From that point forward we became ardent 49ers fans and have had season tickets even to this point. Since we now live in Carson City, I turned the tickets over to my son who lives in the Bay Area, with the proviso that we get to go to any game that we want.

Jack had six season tickets in his name. I paid for two of them, and Jerry Hampton paid for the other two for his and his wife Barbara's use. Jack and Jerry were among the first Aerojet employees that I hired when I was starting B.R.I in Sacramento. Jerry was an interesting fellow. Several years before he went to work for Aerojet, he was involved in an industrial accident. His right hand was blown off and his left hand only had three fingers left. He was also blind and deaf for about a year. After he regained his vision and hearing, he was retrained in computer technology, and became highly proficient as a Cobol programmer. One day, when I was making a presentation to some state people about a system I was selling, I noticed that my audience had stopped paying attention to me. They were all watching Jerry who was lighting a cigarette. He held the book of matches with the three fingers on his left hand, separated a match from the book of matches with the hook that had become his right hand, lit the match with the hook, and lit the cigarette. Quite a show! After the meeting

I told Jerry that if he ever pulled that trick on me again, I would see to it that his hook was placed firmly up his ass.

The Hamptons had a Volkswagen bus that the six of us would take to the football games at Candlestick Park. We would assemble at a local bar and drink some Bloody Marys before the drive to San Francisco. The bus had a little kitchen, and the six of us would have breakfast and some more drinks before arriving in the parking lot. Once at the game we would keep the beer salesmen busy until halftime when we would visit the stadium club for more drinks. By the end of the game I was so blitzed that I didn't know who we were playing much less the score. None of us were in shape to drive home, but drive we did. They say that God takes care of fools and drunks. Well, He certainly took care of us foolish drunks.

One time when the Volkswagen was being serviced, we took my car to the game. After the football game, we stopped for dinner on the way back to Sacramento. Halfway through dinner, Jerry said he was tired and that he would go take a nap in the car and we could meet him later. The rest of us finished our dinner and went out to my car, but Jerry was nowhere in sight. We searched all over the parking lot without success so there was nothing we could do but continue back home without Jerry.

We found out later that Jerry had gotten into the back seat of the wrong car and fell asleep. He woke up and sat up right before the car entered Sacramento. The driver and his passenger let out a shriek and almost had an accident upon seeing this monster with a hook rising up behind them.

We continued this pattern of behavior for a while until Bobbie, rightfully so, said that we were destined to kill ourselves and some innocent people as well if we continued drinking and driving. I was reluctant, at first, to drive separately because we'd had a lot of laughs and fun in that Volkswagen, but Bobbie prevailed, and that's when we discovered Pacifica. We would drive to Pacifica the night before the game, stay at a lovely little motel right on the beach, have dinner, and take a public bus back and forth to the game on Sunday. A much better way to go!

Till 1980, the 49ers were a pretty lousy team. In 1980, however, they won the conference championship and were invited to play for the Super Bowl championship at the Silverdome in Pontiac, Michigan. A lottery determined which of the lucky season ticket holders would be able to buy Super bowl tickets. All six of our tickets were in Jack's name and he was a lucky winner of two tickets to the game. Naturally, I thought that we should have a mini-lottery among the three couples to see which couple would go to the Super Bowl. Jack thought otherwise. He declared himself the winner and went to Michigan to see the 49ers win their first ever Super Bowl. The following year, I arranged to have my tickets transferred to my own name.

It took until 1988 for my name to be selected. Bobbie and I went to Florida to see Super Bowl XXIII when San Francisco beat the Cincinnati Bengals in one of the most thrilling games we had ever seen. That was the game where our quarterback, Joe Montana, with less than a minute to go, drove his team the length of the field for the winning touchdown.

In March of 1972, shortly after we moved into our new home on Great Falls Way, Bobbie got a phone call from her sister, Fla, who had dreadful news. Their sister Fran had been in an accident and was not expected to survive. When Fran was a very young woman, she sang and danced professionally as a showgirl. She performed with Frank Sinatra at the same small club in New Jersey where Sinatra's career began. Fran loved to dance and since Eddie, her husband, didn't care to dance, she had several partners over the years who would take her dancing on weekends. Her last partner, Gordon, who was recently separated from his wife, invited Fran over to see his new apartment after their Friday night dance. Unfortunately, Fran reluctantly agreed, and once at his apartment he tried to rape her and started to rip her clothes off. She ran out of his apartment half naked, trying to escape from him. Gordon got into his car and chased after her, until he caught up with her and ultimately murdered her by running her over with his car. He was later tried and convicted of murder and sentenced to jail for a number of years.

Bobbie, of course, flew back to New York to be with her family and attend the funeral, and I stayed home to take care of the kids. Nina was in a nursing home on Long Island and since Fla was living in Florida, the only visitors that Nina had were Fran and her daughter, Linda. We decided that it would be better for Nina if we moved her back to Sacramento and put her in a local nursing home where Bobbie and I and our kids could spend time with her.

I called Dr. Nittler, our family physician, and asked his advice as to what he thought were the best nursing homes in the area. He recommended a place called Mt. Olivet and I took care of all the arrangements necessary for admitting her. When Bobbie and Nina returned from New York, I met their plane and we drove Nina straight to Mt. Olivet where she lived until her passing in November of 1974, a sad day for the entire family. While she lived there, we would visit as often as possible and would often take her home for Sunday and holiday meals that she thoroughly enjoyed.

Once we had returned to Sacramento from L.A., Bobbie decided that she wanted to continue her education. She enrolled in the PHD program as an English major at the University of California in Davis. She got her Master's degree and almost completed the PHD program when she discovered that she would not be eligible to teach at the university because there was a rule that precluded the university from hiring their own graduates. As a graduate student, however, she was allowed, as a teaching assistant, to teach Freshman English and Introduction to Literature. She also volunteered her time at American River College, teaching Remedial Writing and Bonehead English.

In order to attend the university, the students had to be among the best, (the top 12 1/2 percent) in their high school graduating class. Bobbie would let me read the papers that she brought home to grade. I was astounded that these supposedly bright students couldn't spell, did not know grammatical structure, and could not put two sentences together. I knew Bobbie was a good teacher because at the end of the semester, there was a dramatic improvement in their writing skills.

Bobbie quit the PHD program although she only had to complete her dissertation in order to earn a PHD in English literature. Because she was precluded from teaching at the university and not wanting to teach at the junior college or high school level, she decided to test out the market place and see what type of career might be available to a mature woman holding a masters degree in English. To that end, she took the Federal Service Entrance Exam in 1974 and, as expected, scored extremely well.

A few months after she took the exam, Bobbie received a letter from the Internal Revenue Service. Before she opened the letter, I thought that, damn it, the IRS was after us again. What the letter contained however, was an offer for Bobbie to come to San Francisco and be interviewed for a position as an auditor for the IRS. Although this was a far cry from teaching English literature, we both felt that she should interview with the Federal Government since our brother-in-law, Dave, had a marvelous career working for the Feds. She was offered the job with the proviso that she had to successfully complete a three- month training program conducted in San Francisco. Bobbie accepted the offer and this was the start of her twelve-year career with the Internal Revenue Service.

When Jerry and I first started our dry-cleaning business, we sent the shirts that we took in with the dry-cleaning to a number of different commercial laundries for processing. The one that seemed to be the best was located right in West Sacramento, just a few minutes from where our cleaners was located. We had a neat arrangement with the owners of the laundry. They would do our shirts and we would dry clean the clothing that they took in. This was the laundry that Jerry and I bought, and what a mistake that was! When the owners presented their Profit and Loss statement they neglected to include the cost of management since they ran it as a Mom and Pop business and took their money under the table.

Jerry and I hired a manager to run the laundry and it soon became apparent that we were literally losing our shirts. We let Rick, our manager, go, and after a month of me getting up at 4a.m. to start up the laundry, I had a lot of incentive to get rid of this bad investment. We hired a lawyer who got the contract of sale rescinded and Mom and Pop got their laundry back much to my relief.

Despite this bad investment, the rest of our business was prosperous enough to support two families but becoming rich was out of the question. We did not pay ourselves big salaries but we had all the perks of small business ownership such as company cars, insurance, etc. Any extra money that we had, we invested, along with a friend of ours from the Aerojet days, Bob Miller, in rental property at South Lake Tahoe. In time, we had five or six properties that provided extra income as well as some diversity to our business.

Bobbie started her three-month training program for the IRS towards the end of 1974. She would either drive or take the bus to San Francisco on Monday morning and return home on Friday evening. Her fellow trainees were a great group of guys and gals and after class they would go out for dinner prior to preparing their assignments for the next day's classes. Occasionally, I would meet her in San Francisco for the weekend, but, more often than not, Bobbie wanted to come home to be with the kids and me.

Sometime in November, Nina got very sick from an infection and had to be transferred from Mt. Olivet to a hospital. Since Bobbie was in San Francisco during the week, I would visit Nina on a daily basis and on weekends we both would go to the hospital. Unfortunately, the doctors could not cure this infection and poor Nina died at the age of eighty-two in November 1974.

Our oldest daughter, Ann, went to high school at Saint Francis in Sacramento. We sent Ann to this school, not because she was Catholic, but because it had the reputation of being one of the best schools in the county. Ann received the highest scores on her admission exams and the principal expected great things from her academically. I don't believe she was challenged enough and she kind of drifted through high school with passing but not outstanding grades

Like a lot of teenagers, she wanted to be on her own when she graduated from high school in 1976. I bought her a classic Mustang as a graduation present so she could have some independence. Because she was not interested in going to college I found a job for her, through a friend of mine, working in one of South Lake Tahoe's hotel-casinos as a maid. Bobbie and I thought this was pretty ironic since we could never make her keep her room neat and clean. We also thought that she would realize that working as a maid was not for her and that she would want to reconsider going to college. Well, we were wrong! She liked the casino life and as soon as she was old enough, she transferred from the housekeeping department and became a Keno runner.

When Gerald Ford was President the real estate market was stagnant. In order to stimulate the economy, he signed legislation that allowed a $2,000.00 tax credit for the purchase of a new home. After Ann left home in 1976, we decided that we could live in a smaller house, and in order to take advantage of this tax credit we sold our home on Great Falls Way. We bought a beautiful condominium on Bluff Lane in Fair Oaks, a suburb of Sacramento. Each condo consisted of four units with varying floor plans. Ours was all the way at the end of the road and, being on a bluff, we had a spectacular view from our living room and deck of the American River and the valley behind us.

Our next-door neighbor when we first moved in was Buzz Oates, a builder, and one of the richest men in Sacramento. His teenage daughter drove a Corvette that my teenage daughter, Tracy, lusted over. Buzz was only there for a few months while his mansion was being constructed. He apparently sold his unit and a few weeks after he moved out a very good-looking woman with a young daughter moved in. We exchanged hellos and she told me her name was Susan Brauner and her daughter's name was Lisa. That evening as Bobbie and I were having cocktails on our back deck, we couldn't help but overhear the conversation coming from Susan's deck

A man had moved into Susan's condo that afternoon and from his accent I thought he was French. Their conversation was the strangest that we had ever heard. Here, he had moved in with her, and he was asking questions like what she did for a living and did she have any brothers and sisters. She in turn was asking him similar questions that indicated that they did not know much about one another, and yet they were living together. We found out later that they had just recently met and decided to buy the condo as an investment. Susan had no intention of letting Raymond live there but Raymond had other ideas. It turns out Raymond was from a very wealthy family in Chile and he was so charming that Susan let him sleep in the spare bedroom that night; that arrangement lasted for exactly one evening.

Raymond Valdes was one of the most fascinating characters that I have ever met. He reminded me a lot of my father. He was charming, had a great sense of humor, and was one hundred percent con artist. The Bluffs had a recreational area consisting of a club-house, swimming pool, and two tennis courts. Raymond and I became tennis buddies and would spend countless hours after work and on weekends playing tennis with other members of the Bluffs. Susan, Raymond, Bobbie and I became close friends. A little too close, as a matter of fact. Frequently I would come home from work only to find Raymond sitting in my living-room waiting for me.

When we first met, Susan was a principal of a local high school and Raymond, although not working, had plenty of money. About twice a year his parents would send him an infusion of cash. The Lincoln Continental car that he was driving would suddenly turn into a Rolls Royce, and we would be taken out to expensive restaurants for dinner where Raymond always paid the bill in cash. When his funds started to run low, Raymond was not embarrassed to borrow money from me and he always paid it back when the next infusion arrived. I understand that other friends of his were not as fortunate as I was in getting repaid.

Raymond got involved in several different business enterprises. The most notable one was The Sacramento Telephone Company. When the telephone industry was first deregulated, anyone who had the necessary capital could start their own phone company. Raymond induced several prominent Sacramento businessmen to invest in his company, which was wildly successful at first. I visited Raymond's office when he first started this business. He had a huge private office that had a full bar, a large television set, and expensive furniture. I thought that this reminded me of Ron Morrison and how not to succeed in business. I was right, and a few years after starting the Sacramento Telephone Company, the original backers kicked Raymond out in order to protect their investments.

By 1976, I was getting pretty bored with the Fabricare business. I decided to see if I could get back into selling computer services and I came up with a concept that, although unique, would be easy to implement. I thought that there must be many companies located in the central part of the country and on the east coast that did not have offices out west but would like to sell their products and services to west coast clients. I did some research, sent out letters offering my services, and received a surprisingly good response.

I took a flying trip across the country and the end result was that I signed contracts with seven companies to act as their west coast representative at a retainer of $100.00 each per week. The companies were Arcola Software, Arcola Illinois, Computer Horizons, New York, New York, Franklin Data Services, Springfield, Illinois, Pensurdata, Philadelphia, Pennsylvania, Personnel Data Systems, Conshohocken, Pennsylvania, Real-Time Computer Systems Inc., Bridgeport, Connecticut, and Sartoris Public Systems, Carmichael, California.

I formed a company, Computer Management Systems Marketing, and rented a desk from my good friend Harris Herman who had leased the penthouse in the Crocker Bank Building for his company, Software Module Marketing, Inc. I had worked with Harris in the B.R.I. days and he formed his company after B.R.I. collapsed; however he was still selling the same software that B.R.I. had developed. Harris and his wife Carole struggled for many years while they grew their business until they finally struck gold by selling their company for several million dollars to Sterling Software of Dallas, Texas.

After a few months, Harris needed the space that I was using so I rented an office on 21st Street in downtown Sacramento. Although I was very successful in selling the concept of marketing for these seven companies, I failed miserably in obtaining any business for them. I tried darned hard to sell their products and services to my clients without any success. In retrospect, what I should have done was hire a team of commissioned salesmen and have each one of them concentrate on one product or service rather than trying to do it all by myself. The closest I came to selling anything was forming a joint venture between Sartoris and Computer Horizons. We put a proposal together for a million dollar computer system for the Department of Rehabilitation. I thought we had the inside track on getting a contract because my neighbor and friend, Don Trujillo, was one of the department's managers who I believed would be the decision maker. Well, I was wrong. The award went to Computer Sciences which was marketing its system to Don's boss, so we really never had a chance to win.

Eventually, my retainers dried up because of my lack of success in selling anything for the seven firms that were paying me. In order to keep my company afloat, I changed gears and took a different approach. I started to sell studies to various state agencies where I had contacts. I would staff these projects with independent contractors who were willing to wait to get paid when I got paid from my clients because I did not have the ability to support a payroll.

My old friend from the War-on-Poverty days, Marion Woods, was now head of Welfare for the State of California under Governor Jerry Brown. The name of the department back then was the Department of Benefit Payments. I sold Marion a $50,000.00 project called "Job Creation through Economic Development." We completed the project in June of 1977 and our study was well received and several of our recommendations were implemented. What was interesting about this contract that was during the course of the project, the Los Angeles Times was investigating the department's method of awarding contracts. The investigative reporter found out about my contract and was about to write a scandalous article about why a drycleaner, who happened to be a friend of the department head, was awarded this type of project. When the reporter contacted me about this suspicious contract, I confessed to being a drycleaner, but also informed him that I had a Bachelor of Science degree, a law degree, and twenty years in the consulting business. That put an end to that story.

Mentioning Governor Jerry Brown reminded me of a rather amusing event that took place when I was working for B.R.I. I used to take the midnight flyer between Sacramento and Los Angeles on a frequent basis. One evening, as I boarded the plane I saw an individual wearing a rather seedy looking jacket but with a familiar face sitting in the window seat. Being the consummate salesman, I sat next to him and said:

"Sir, you look very familiar and I wonder if I met you while I was doing some consulting for the State of California?"

"Well, that's possible," he said. " My name is Pat Brown and I used to be the Governor of California."

"Oh my God! Can I buy you a drink, sir?"

"Yes you may. Please tell the stewardess that I'll have a very dry martini."

I also had a martini and on the rest of the trip to Sacramento, he told me of his plans for helping his son, Jerry Brown, in his campaign to become Secretary of State for California. What a nice guy he was, and a gentleman to boot.

There was another "goodie" associated with buying a condominium at the Bluffs. In order to stimulate sales of their units, the builder's offered as an incentive round-trip airline tickets for two to any place you wanted to go within the continental United States. Because Fla and Dave were living in Coral Gables, we decided to go to Florida. Back then, when you purchased a roundtrip ticket going from coast to coast you were permitted to stop over in two cities on the way back. We selected New Orleans and Las Vegas.

Dave had been Commissioner of Customs and had had jurisdiction over all the ports and airports in that part of the country. Now retired from the federal service, he was a consultant to the cruise lines. As a courtesy to Dave, they would often provide free cruises for him and Fla when their ships were not fully booked. As a surprise to us, Dave got cabins on a four-day cruise to the Bahamas for all of us on the Sunward II, an NCL cruise ship.

I hadn't been on a cruise ship since I was a little boy and I remembered getting very seasick on the *Normandy* on the way back from France to New York City. My only other experience at sea was on a troop ship going from Japan to Korea where I was again seasick. Sometimes when we were sightseeing in Sausalito, California, we would stroll through the shops on the Trade Fair, an old ferry that was permanently moored to a dock. (It is no longer there.) I would start to feel some motion sickness and would have to leave the shops and get back on shore.

Because of these experiences, I was not a happy camper when I found out what Dave and Fla had planned for us. However, since the price was right (free), I didn't put up too much of an argument. We had a marvelous time during those four days and I didn't even think about getting sick. As a matter of fact, Bobbie and I got hooked on cruising and have enjoyed thirteen or fourteen cruises since then.

We lived at the Bluffs for about eighteen months when we decided it was time to move again. There were many reasons behind our decision to move back into a house. The condo was really too small for a family that had two teenage kids. Also, the Homeowners Association had lots of restrictive rules such as not allowing you to park on the street even for a few minutes when you were unloading your car, etc. Another problem was that Raymond believed that my condo was merely an extension of his own. I would show up at odd times only to find Raymond in my living room or on my deck. Now, I liked Raymond a whole bunch but I really did not want him to be my roommate.

We found a lovely older house on La Mirada Circle in Fair Oaks that was truly more suitable for a family with teenagers. We sold our condo in a matter of days and made a nice $30,000.00 profit that was not bad for the short period of time that we lived in it. We bought the house on La Mirada, which also had a lovely view from the back deck. When we moved in, the deck was covered with tarpaper, and Raymond came over and helped me surface it with wood. Because we were a few miles from the Bluffs, I was not overly concerned about Raymond's constant presence.

After living in the house for a short period, we noticed some strange happenings. Bobbie would put a broom away in the broom closet on the right side and the next day she would find it on the left side. When we were having dinner with the kids in the downstairs family room, we would hear doors opening and closing up stairs, although no one was up there. One time after Bobbie went shopping, she left a bag of groceries on the kitchen counter while she went out to the car for the rest of the provisions. When she came back inside, she noticed that a box of cereal that she had just bought was open, still upright on the counter, but most of the flakes had spilled out of the box and were on the floor. I was at work and the kids were in school so she couldn't imagine what had happened.

That evening our next-door neighbors, the Adornos, invited us over for some wine. Cathy asked us how we were enjoying living in our new home, and Bobbie, laughingly said, "We think it's haunted." Cathy looked shocked, and than asked if we knew about the history of the house. About fifteen years earlier it was being built to be the dream home of a prominent local builder and his wife. About a day or two after they moved into their dream home the wife was involved in an automobile accident that killed her. The husband moved out and sold it to another couple that also had a tragic misfortune. At a party one evening one of their guests thought it would be fun to swing out from their deck at the end of a rope and swing back in. He misjudged the distance, crashed into a tree, and was instantly killed.

Cathy told us that nobody ever lived in our house for more than eighteen months because they all experienced things very similar to what we were experiencing. We became convinced that the house was haunted but because we were very comfortable there we decided to tough it out for a while.

If anyone was to ask any of my friends if John Silberman believed in the supernatural or ghosts, they would say, "You are nuts." I am perceived to be a very rational, no nonsense, practical kind of guy with little tolerance for the make believe.

Bobbie and I had another experience that made believers out of us. In 1997 we decided to spend our fortieth anniversary in Tonopah, Nevada. We reserved a suite at the old Mizpah hotel that had a reputation for being haunted. After a delightful dinner in the hotel restaurant, we retired to our rooms to exchange gifts, which we did. When we got up the next morning we went into the living room area only to discover that the wrapping paper that had contained our gifts were on the other side of the room from where we had left them the night before. Also, Bobbie, who still smokes, found her cigarette pack also across the room with several cigarettes missing. The door to our suite was locked and bolted so nobody could have come in while we were sleeping and the living room windows were closed so there was no wind to blow things across the room. There were other peculiarities as well. The only illogical explanation that we could come up with was that we had been visited by the ghost that dwells in the Mizpah hotel.

One afternoon while we were sitting on our deck, I received a distressing phone call from my sister. Our father had suffered a heart attack and was taken by ambulance to the hospital. While we were making arrangements to fly back east, I received another call from Pat who informed me that Dad had had a second heart attack and had died. This was on July 1st, 1979. I was devastated by this news. Not only did I love him as my father, but also I greatly admired him for his many interests and accomplishments in life. Although Dad never graduated from high school, he was the most educated man I ever knew. When I was studying Latin at Bordentown, he would write me letters in Latin that I had to have my teacher translate for me. He was an inventor and brilliant businessman who held many patents for the machines that manufactured zippers. He produced two shows on Broadway, a revival of *R.U.R.* and a play *What Big Ears You Have.* In 1946, he published a book *A United States of Europe or Else* where he predicted a common currency for European nations, fifty-six years before it actually happened.

Over his lifetime, my dad made and lost fortunes. He was a compulsive gambler who could not stand prosperity. After making another million he would say, "I guess I pulled another rabbit out of the hat." Unfortunately, he died in one of his periodic down periods, leaving his wife, my beloved stepmother, Ida, with very little to live on for the rest of her life. We took the red-eye that night for his funeral, and that was the first time I cried since I was a little boy.

On our way back from Florida, after our first cruise, we stopped for a few days in New Orleans before heading to Las Vegas and home. In New Orleans, Bobbie bought some very colorful dresses and blouses in a shop where "one size fits all." On many occasions while wearing these items, not only did she receive wonderful compliments, but also inquiries as to where they could be bought. Because this type of clothing was not being sold in Sacramento, she thought that if she opened a dress shop that featured these garments they would sell like hot cakes.

Also, she was getting a little burnt out with the IRS. After almost five years she was one of the top auditors and had acted as a supervisor on several occasions. The IRS management would not promote her because she would not play their stupid bureaucratic games. When interviewed for promotion, she would answer their questions truthfully, and refused to give them the politically correct answers. That, combined with the government's emphasis on promoting minorities, limited her future with the IRS.

Thus, in 1997 Bobbie's Backroom Boutique was born. She resigned from the IRS and found a location on 2nd Street in Old Sacramento for her shop. She did all the planning, all the decorating and ordered the first shipment of clothing from New Orleans. Her store was beautiful and she received lots of compliments from the neighboring merchants. Because of the store's uniqueness, it was featured on a local TV show. Because Old Sacramento was a tourist attraction, in addition to locals, her customers were from all over this country and other countries, as well. The store did extremely well until the economy took a dive.

Jimmy Carter, our Nobel Prize winning ex-President, came into office in 1977. It didn't take too long before his team of incompetent economic advisers put our economy in the tank. Inflation was running rampant, with interest rates on home mortgages exceeding 17 percent, and credit card interest rates of over 20 percent. This played hell with our business. New construction dried up and without new apartments being built, the mainstay of our business, selling drapes, was seriously impacted. Jerry and I started to sell off our Lake Tahoe investments to keep our business afloat. In hindsight, that was probably a mistake as we probably should have kept our property and folded the business.

Bobbie's business suffered as well. About 80 percent of her sales were on credit cards, and with interest rates as high as they were, people stopped using their credit cards. It got to the point where she only made enough to cover the rent and pay her part-time employees and there was nothing left over for her. She arranged a deal with another merchant which allowed her to cut back on half her rent and eliminate one part-time employee in the hope that the economy would improve.

To make matters even worse for us financially, Bobbie and I had committed to having a house built in El Dorado Hills. We had bought a lot almost directly across from the house that Susan and Raymond had bought after they sold their condo at the Bluffs. When we made the decision to have the house built, we had no idea that our fortunes would become as bad as they did. We moved into the house when it was completed in 1979 and the first thing we did was to put a "For Sale" sign on our front lawn.

The first night in the new house we had a couple of rather distressing occurrences. I had borrowed one of our trucks that our businesses used for delivering drapes because it had racks installed which made the moving of our clothing a snap. Because we had our two cars in the garage and Tracy's car in the driveway, I had to leave the truck on the street overnight. When I got up in the morning, I discovered that someone, and I suspect it was my neighbor on the right, had released the brake on the truck and pushed it down the hill. Not a very neighborly act! The second annoyance occurred when our neighbor on the left, a retired marine colonel, came over to our house in the late evening, not to introduce himself but to complain about our dog's barking. This neighbor, Brooks, once he found out our telephone number, would call Bobbie and complain about the slightest little thing. Whenever I answered the phone, however, this coward would back down completely.

One evening after coming home from work, I checked my mailbox and discovered a brown paper sack. I took it in the house and said to Bobbie, "Somebody sent us a present." I opened it to find a present of dog shit and a note from Brooks telling me to keep my dog off his lawn. I told Bobbie that I was going over to kill that son-of-a-bitch right now! She, Tracy, and Patrick urged me to calm down and if, after twenty-four hours had passed, I was still upset, then I could go kill the bastard. The next day, I called the US Post Office and asked if they had any rules about someone putting dog shit in my mailbox. I was told that this appeared to be a neighborhood quarrel and they would have no part of it.

When I got home that evening I wasn't feeling the slightest bit less hostile about my asshole neighbor who had the gall to put a bag full of shit in my mailbox. I promised my family that I would not kill Brooks but that I intended to beat him to within one inch of his life. I went next door and rang his doorbell. A fairly unattractive woman, who was reeking of alcohol, answered it.

"Who are you?" she asked

"I am your next door neighbor who received a lovely present from your husband yesterday and I'm here to thank him," I replied

"He is busy now and can't come to the door."

"Well, you tell that cowardly son-of-a-bitch that if he ever pulls that trick again I will knock your front door in and make him confront me. I thought Brooks was supposed to be an officer and a gentleman, but I can tell you that he is not. My dog will not be confined and will jump off my deck to be free. If she poops on your lawn, all you have to do is tell me, or my wife, and we will clean it up. Is that clear?"

"Yes sir, I will tell him."

I went home feeling better, but not much. Brooks and Joann were thorns in our sides for the seventeen years that we lived in El Dorado Hills. I think they were either crazy or were a couple of drunks, or both. One day Brooks would bring roses from his rose garden to Bobbie, and the next day he would be calling her complaining about something one or another of us had done. He hated to have cars parked on the street, but with a two-car garage, and four cars (just for that first year), what were we to do? He barely tolerated that, knowing that our adult kids would be leaving soon. After they were gone, any of our guest's cars parked on the street for more than 12 hours would have their tires slashed, or be egged under cover of night.

Financially, for us, things were going from bad to worse. We never should have bought the house in El Dorado Hills, but fortunately we were able to rent our house on La Mirada to people who eventually purchased it from us. Bobbie kept Bobbie's Backdoor Boutique in operation for as long as possible but she finally had to shut it down and return the leftover garments to her supplier in New Orleans. Luckily, she applied for and was reinstated as an auditor for the IRS. She became the family's sole breadwinner because Fabricare could no longer afford to pay me a salary.

Jerry and I shut down our drapery manufacturing business and returned the leased sewing machines to our supplier. We were stuck with a large inventory of fabric that we had to pay for personally because the thought of bankruptcy was abhorrent to us. We sold our drapery cleaning business for pennies on the dollar and were left with just two cleaning plants that could hardly support two families. We agreed that Jerry would continue on with the business while I looked for a job because I still had a lot of contacts in the consulting and computer businesses.

Once again, I was reminded of how, when you are successfully employed, returned calls were the norm, and when you were unemployed, your supposed friends and associates forget about you. I did manage to get a breakfast appointment with the managing partner of Peat Marwick in order to discuss job opportunities. I had not quite finished my orange juice when it became painfully apparent that his consulting firm had no use for a fifty-year old salesman. Since he was paying, I decided to have steak and eggs and annoyed him thoroughly by telling some of the worst jokes that I knew.

After several months of networking, I finally got a call from my old buddy, Bruce Joplin, President of Sartoris Public Systems. Bruce told me that Boeing Computer Services was looking for a manager for its Sacramento office and that I should contact Tom Guilfoil about the opening. Within a few days, I met with Tom, a really likable fellow, who was about my age so that was not a problem that I would have to deal with. Tom was the acting manager of the Sacramento office for Boeing Computer Services, and one of his tasks was to find a suitable local replacement for himself so that he could return to Seattle where his home was. Tom and I hit it off really well, and although he did not have the authority to hire me, he was able to arrange a trip for me to Seattle where I would be interviewed by several of the Boeing executives.

I purchased a fashionable three-piece green polyester suit for this occasion, not knowing that Washingtonians were into "natural fabrics only." I spent two grueling days at Boeing being interviewed by no less than seven of their executives. Early in the process, I learned to say as little as possible and to express much interest at their egotistical presentations. At any rate, I survived the interviews, flew back home and prayed that they would hire me as I was now tapped out on all my credit cards.

Chapter Nine
Boeing Computer Services

1980 - 1982

November 7, 1980

Mr. John K. Silberman
3501 Ridgeview Drive
El Dorado Hills CA 95630

Dear Mr. Silberman:

We are pleased to confirm your acceptance of the offer extended to you for the position of Computing Consultant with the Boeing Computer Services Company, located in our Sacramento, California office. We understand that you will be joining the Boeing Company effective November 17, 1980. The beginning annual salary is $44,500.00 based on a standard work year of 2.088 hours.

We welcome your decision to become a member of management with the Boeing Computer Services Company and wish you every success in your assignment.

Sincerely,

Carl H. Hough
Manager
Professional Placement

"Thank God, dear, that I have a job again. Between our two salaries we should be able to make ends meet and pay off all our debts within a year or so. I guess that despite the green polyester suit, my bullshit saved the day for us. As my dad would say, 'I pulled another rabbit out of the hat!' "

Once I started working for B.C.S. (Boeing Computer Services), Tom Guilfoil took me around to the State Departments he was working with and introduced me to their managers, many of whom I knew from my old B.R.I. days. Tom had just completed an organizational study of the Health and Welfare Data Center and one of his recommendations was that the deputy, Phil Mendes, should replace the department's chief, Russ Bohart. I attended the meeting where Tom presented his findings and recommendations to Mario Obledo, the agency head that Russ Bohart reported to. Mario rejected this particular recommendation although he implemented many of Tom's other suggestions.

After Tom went back to Seattle, I tried on many occasions to get an appointment with Russ without any success. Boeing was clearly on Russ's shitlist for trying to remove him from his job. After several months Russ finally agreed to meet with me for lunch where I discovered his fondness for white wine. Now Russ was a great big guy, probably about three hundred pounds, who could drink white wine like it was water. I tried to keep up with him, but only succeeded in getting smashed. Luckily, the restaurant was near my office so I could walk back to work and sleep it off. After several similar lunches with Russ, Boeing was in his good graces again. I had opened the door for more consulting work within his department, at the risk of turning myself into a wino.

Before Tom went back home to Seattle, he sat me down in his office and offered me some advice on how to proceed within the B.C.S organization. In the first place, he suggested that I toss my new green, three-piece polyester suit, and replace it with a woolen suit, preferable black with some faint pin stripes. Next he cautioned that my colorful argyle socks would have to go. Boeing management only wore black socks and never brown shoes. I thought that Tom must have been kidding until I attended my first Boeing management meeting in Seattle. I looked around the sea of black pin striped suits sporting black socks and wondered what I had gotten myself into.

My first assignment after being hired by B.C.S. was to attend a three-day seminar in San Francisco on the use and value of various database systems, such as Adabas, etc. My boss, Daryl Perkins, knew that I had been out of touch with the technology for a few years and that I needed to get up to speed again. I knew the honeymoon was over when the room Boeing provided for me in San Francisco was located at the local Y.M.C.A. When I was in Seattle, during the interview process, I had stayed at a four-star hotel and was wined and dined at first-class restaurants. But now, to get to my room at the "Y", I had to pass through the lobby where a group of old men were sitting, half of them with drool cascading down their chins. My room had a single bed with a bare bulb above it, and a bathroom that I was afraid to use.

The seminar was designed for individuals who were much more technical than I was so I really didn't understand much of what was presented. I did, however learn a lot of new buzzwords which would become useful to me in the future. After the first night, I checked out of the "Y" and moved to a more suitable hotel and paid the difference in cost out of my own pocket.

Although I was the manager of the Sacramento office for B.C.S., I had less decision-making authority than my former secretary at B.R.I. had had. All decisions of any type, including the hiring of staff, were made at headquarters in Seattle. I found this out early on in the game, when my old friend Marion Woods, head of Benefit Payments, asked me to write a proposal for some automated system that his department needed. I interviewed his staff and determined what the requirements were for the system. Based on what I had found out, I wrote what I considered to be a pretty darn good proposal. Because

I did not have the authority to sign the proposal, I had to send it up to headquarters in Seattle for approval. What they sent back to me had no resemblance to what Marion's department needed. When I called my boss to complain he told me that they were the experts and that in the future I should not waste my time writing proposals. What I should do, he said, was to find out what the department's needs were and his group of expert proposal writers would take it from there.

With a great deal of embarrassment, I delivered the proposal to my friend Marion who called me a few days later to ask if I had taken leave of my senses. I tried to explain to him that the "experts" in Seattle thought that the system should be designed as proposed and that he would be happy with the results. He flat out laughed at me and invited me to have a drink with him after work where I could tell him what really happened, which I did.

I did not have to worry about losing too many more clients and friends because after about three months on the job, I got a call from Daryl notifying me that I was being laid off. Although he told me I was doing a fine job, I was the new kid on the block and during Boeing's periodic downturns he applied the LIFO method of inventory control, Last In First Out. While I didn't much like my job, this was devastating news, because I really needed the salary.

The Boeing office, located on Richards Blvd. in Sacramento, was staffed with Jay Johnston, sales; Tony VanWolferin, programming; Judi, administrative assistant, and me. While I worked for Daryl who was in charge of consulting, the other three worked for John Kopas who was in charge of sales for the West Coast. Jay and I had become good friends during those first few months. We played racquetball against each other and had lunch together frequently. Although Jay and his wife, Missy, were about twenty years younger than we were, Bobbie and I really enjoyed their company. When Jay found out that I was going to be laid off, he proposed a solution for me. He said that he would ask his boss, John Kopas, if he could transfer to technical support, where he had previously worked, and that would leave an opening in sales for me.

We met with John in San Francisco the following day, and John agreed to Jay's suggestion as long as his boss, Jack Bunnis, would concur. Jack, who had graduated from Fort Benning O.C.S. liked my background and approved of the transfer. I will forever owe a debt of gratitude to Jay Johnston for saving my ass from what could have been a personal financial catastrophe.

The first thing John did was to send me back to Vienna, Virginia, for a two-week course designed to teach the new Boeing salesmen about the various engineering products and services that Boeing offered, and how to sell them. The instruction was very intense and lasted ten hours a day with enough homework to keep you up till the early hours of the morning. Most of the Boeing students were in their mid-twenties to early thirties, so it was natural for them, as well as the instructors, to call on me for advice or to demonstrate a particular selling technique. It seemed strange to be back in a classroom after so many years, but I had a powerful motivation, a paycheck, that kept me going.

On the weekend between the two weeks of classes, I had nothing special to do, so I decided to rent a car and drive to Atlantic City to see what the city was like now that gambling was legal. When Bobbie and I were first married, after Ann was born, we would occasionally spend a weekend in Atlantic City where we could be by ourselves and enjoy walking along the famous boardwalk. Well, things had certainly changed. I drove into the city and tried to check into several of the casino hotels only to be told, that although there were plenty of rooms, I had to pay for two nights, instead of the one night that was all I wanted.

I drove back out of the city and about ten miles away I checked into some sleaze-bag motel where, in addition to an outrageous rate, I also had to leave a deposit for my room key. I went back into Atlantic City, where two more unpleasant experiences awaited me. I found out that I had to pay for parking if I parked in one of the casino parking lots. This was a surprise to me as parking was always free at the Nevada casinos.

The next surprise came when I was playing at a $5.00 blackjack table, and the pit boss came over and changed the minimum bet to

$25.00. I left that table in search of another $5.00 limit game without success. I grabbed a bite to eat, drove back to my fleabag of a motel, went to sleep, and couldn't wait to get back to Vienna for the next week of classes. I don't regret having gone to Atlantic City; it's just something that I never have to do again.

During the middle of 1980, my sister called me with some very distressing news. Hiwa had developed cancer, and despite some aggressive chemotherapy treatments, she was not expected to live too much longer. She was living with my sister, and on several occasions, Bobbie and I would fly back to New York to visit with her and provide moral support to Pat. She died on February 21, 1981, the first of my three mothers to go.

When I transferred from consulting to sales, Boeing adjusted my base salary downward slightly. I was now eligible to participate in their sales incentive program. Each month for the next twelve months that I worked for Boeing, I would receive a ten to fifteen page computer printout that was my commission statement. Sometimes the statement was accompanied by a check and sometimes it wasn't. Nobody, during that entire period of time, could explain to me what my commission was based on. I swore that if I was ever in a position to establish a commission plan that I would ensure that it was simple, understandable, and achievable. I subsequently did have that opportunity.

I was fairly successful as a Boeing salesman, and at one of our quarterly sales meetings, I even won a prize. Jack Bunnis called me up to the podium where I faced a sea of dark pin-striped suits and black socks. Jack presented me with a treasure chest that contained chocolates covered with gold foil. *Wow*, I thought, *What a great salesman I am.*

It didn't take me too long to figure out that if I was to have any kind of career at Boeing, I would have to move to Seattle, and that was not an option that I would ever consider. I knew that quitting and looking for a new job was not an option either. So what I did was engage the services of a headhunting firm. The first couple of agencies that I talked to were quite a joke. They asked me questions such as where would I like to see myself in five years and then in ten years. My response was that I would like to see myself breathing which did not make them overly friendly towards me. I finally found a firm that told me that my background was perfect for a company that wanted to establish an office in Sacramento.

The executive recruiter set up a breakfast meeting for me at the Red Lyon Inn with Art Levine, the individual whose company wanted to expand into the Sacramento market place. Art managed the Santa Clara office of Telos Consulting Services, a division of Telos Corporation. Art's clients in the Bay area were aerospace and engineering firms that bought the services of Telos's scientific programmers and engineers. He believed that Sacramento would be a great expansion possibility.

"Art," I said. "There are two flaws in what you want to accomplish in Sacramento. In the first place, with the exception of Aerojet, there is no market for the type of talent that you sell in the Santa Clara arena. Secondly, even if there were such a market here, I am not the right guy to sell these services because I don't have the right technical background."

"John, I appreciate your honesty and frankness, and now why don't you tell me what you think Telos could do in your marketplace?"

I explained to Art that Sacramento, as the capital of the State, was pretty much a government town and what would sell here was business application programmers, a field that Telos was not currently engaged in. We spent several hours that morning talking over various scenarios where my talents and Telos's capabilities might mesh. Art and I really hit it off and he invited me and Bobbie to dinner that evening where we all had a great time. A few days later we met again and discussed salary, start time, office space, etc. Art, who was a pilot and had his own Piper Archer, said he would fly me down to Santa Monica where I would meet the president of his division and some other executives that worked for Telos.

I thought it was a done deal so I prepared a business plan for the Sacramento office of Telos Consulting Services and in my best dark pin-striped suit complete with black socks, flew down with Art to

Santa Monica. We had a great flight and I was thrilled at the opportunity of working for Art in a market place where I knew my talents would shine.

We met Dick Brewer, Dennis Delesio, and a few other Telos executives for lunch at a restaurant close to their corporate office. These guys were all dressed in gym suits so I felt a little out of place in my three-piece dark pin-striped suit complete with black socks and shiny new briefcase containing my business plan. Lunch was a disaster! All these men would talk about was the Laker's basketball team and what their chances were for winning the championship. Every time I tried to bring business into the conversation, the table would become silent. Even Art was strangely quiet.

After lunch we went back to the corporate office where the guys shot basketballs through a hoop while I cooled my heels in Dick's office. Finally Dick came into his office, closed the door, sat behind his desk, and asked me what I wanted.

"Dick, I've prepared a business plan for the Sacramento office of Telos Consulting Services which shows what I can accomplish during my first year and what I project for the following two years, and I'd like to review that plan with you now."

"Why don't you leave it with me and I'll look it over some other time. Is there any thing else that you want to talk to me about?"

"Well yes, Dick. I'd like to verify the salary that Art and I talked about and when you would like for me to start working for Telos."

"John, Art and I talked about you, but no firm decision has been made and if we do open an office in Sacramento that office will report directly to me and not Art."

"Sorry, Dick. I thought I had a job offer and that it was only a formality coming down here to meet with you and the other fellows."

"Let me think about it and I'll call you soon."

Needless to say, the flight back to Sacramento was a pretty chilly affair. I though I had been sandbagged by Art who in turn thought Dick had sandbagged him. I went home that evening thoroughly depressed because I knew that this job was an ideal fit for me. Contemplating the future at Boeing was even gloomier now.

Early on, in my brief career with Boeing Computer Services, Dennis Sechrest, a salesman working for Pro-Data made a sales call on Boeing. What Denny was selling was contract labor (staffing) services. Because Boeing did not require his services, and never contemplating that Denny would be a competitor of mine one day, I opened up my kimono to him. Not only did I tell him the organizations that he should call on, but I also gave him the names and phone numbers of the decision makers in these departments. Pro-Data was in the same business that Telos was in.

A few days after my calamitous trip to Santa Monica, Dick Brewer called me at my office.

"John, let's do it," he said.

"Do what?" I replied.

"I read your business plan and I must confess that's the first business plan I ever read. If you can accomplish what you said you could, you will be a star in my organization. Do you think you can start on March 1st?" (1982)

"Yes sir, and you surely won't regret making this decision."

I immediately called Bobbie and gave her this great news. My starting salary was $48,000.00 per year, an increase over what Boeing was paying me. I gave Boeing two-weeks notice and began what was to be the best experience in my business career.

Chapter Ten
Telos Consulting Services

1982 - 1995

I've always considered myself a very lucky kind of guy. I have a very special definition of what lucky means to me. I don't know whether I read this definition or heard it from someone else, but it is definitely not original with me. "Luck is when opportunity and preparation cross paths." I certainly was lucky when Dick offered me the regional manager's job in Sacramento. It was an opportunity that I was prepared to accept.

I was so excited about getting started that I told Boeing that I would use my vacation for the two-weeks notice that I had given them so I could start working for Telos immediately without being on their payroll. The first thing I did was to contact Russ Waltrip who was then the Director of Information Technology for Sacramento County. Russ used to work for me in many different capacities during my B.R.I days. He told me to contact Jack Watts who worked for him as the manager of Criminal Justice Information Bureau. Jack, my old football buddy, told me that he had two openings for contract programmers in his bureau and gave me the opportunity to fill these two slots.

The very same day that Jack gave me these requirements, I interviewed Doug Kempster who had been referred to me by one of my contacts. Doug was currently working for the Computer Sciences

Corporation and was sick of the traveling that was required of him. He liked what I had to offer and I arranged a dinner meeting for that evening with Jack, Doug, and me. Luckily, Jack and Doug hit it off, and I was able to hire Doug and place him at Sacramento County even before I was on Telos's payroll. Doug was my very first employee for Telos, and years later, he would become my son-in-law and the father of two of my grandchildren.

To fill the second slot at Sacramento County, I interviewed and hired Vicky Dill who had just completed a consulting assignment in Alaska working for Price Waterhouse. I now had three employees working for Telos in Sacramento; Lyle Sherman who Art had placed at Ex-Log Corporation, Doug, and Vicky. Not bad, considering that I had not yet received my first paycheck from my new company.

An old friend of mine, Bob Rutter, once the Managing Partner for Ernst & Ernst, had established an accountancy practice in Old Sacramento. Bob had a spare office that he rented to me for a nominal price. Old Sacramento was a great location for Telos because of its proximity to the State and local agencies with which I would be doing business. It was also a kicky place to have an office. On the first floor there was "Buffalo Bob's Ice Cream Parlor", which Bob Rutter owned at the time. There were also a variety of T-shirt shops and other stores that catered to the tourist trade. This was the area that Bobbie had had her shop, "Bobbie's Backdoor Boutique."

On the second floor of 106 K Street, the building where my office was, there was a secretarial pool that I used for typing and binding my proposals to the government agencies. That is where I first met Jan Cooper (now, Jan Arnold). When Jan got tired of working for the secretarial pool I introduced her to Susan Brauner, my neighbor, who was then working for Blue Diamond as the Public Relations Manager. Jan worked for Blue Diamond for a number of years until she was laid off, a victim of reorganization. I hired Jan and she worked for me for many years and she is still working as my replacement for the company that let me go.

Kate Sandusky was Bob's secretary and, although she did not have sufficient time for me, she was allowed to answer my phone. I eventually hired Kate to be my assistant when my business had grown to the point where I could no longer handle everything by myself. Bob was okay with this and hired more of a bookkeeper to replace Kate.

When I first met Bob Rutter he was your typical straight-laced, candy-assed, three-piece suit accounting manager. Shortly after his divorce, Bob morphed from being the Managing Partner of Ernst & Ernst, and President of the University Club, to Buffalo Bob, Mayor of Old Sacramento, and proprietor of "Buffalo Bob's Ice Cream Parlor." Gone were the three-piece suits, replaced by jeans, T-shirts, and cowboy hats and boots. He limited his accountancy practice to just a few clients so that he had ample time to visit with his scores of friends in the many bars and taverns of Old Sacramento.

In the summertime, Bob liked to sunbathe. He would accomplish this by stripping off all his clothes, sit in his executive chair in front of the window, and enjoy the warm sunshine. Sometimes he would forget to close the door to his office. Invariably when that happened, I would have an interview scheduled with one of my applicants who would have to pass by Bob's office to get to mine. I knew Bob was at it again when my candidate would do a double take before greeting me. Kate, who was unflappable, liked the scenery, I think.

One of the best clients that I had over the years was Sacramento County. I started to do business with them when I worked for Aerojet and continued to do business with them until I was forced to retire in 2002. There were many reasons for my great success with the County, not the least of which was that many of the managers, including the director, had worked for me in the past. One of my business credos is that I always make friends with my employees and clients. Consequently, I had many friends at Sacramento County and that, I believe, gave me a slightly unfair advantage over many of my competitors.

I would do lots of things that were not normally part of my life style in the pursuit of business. Rupert Hess was one of the key managers of Sacramento's Department of Information Technology.

Although Rupe had never worked for me in the past, he and his wife Carol, and Bobbie and I became very good friends. Rupe is a giant of a man, well over six feet tall, and probably about three hundred and fifty pounds. Carol is also a very tall lady.

One day Rupert invited me to go on a fishing trip with him and some of the other members of his department. Not wanting to miss an opportunity to socialize with some of my clients, I accepted his invitation reluctantly, because fishing was on the bottom of my list of things to do. Rupe suggested that I spend the night at his house because we had to get up very early in the morning for our drive to the Bay Area where the fishing boat was moored.

I accepted his invitation, and after a leisurely dinner, Carol retired for the evening while Rupe and I went out in his backyard where we proceeded to drink vast quantities of Vodka and orange juice. Rupe being as big as he was could drink me under the table, which is exactly what he did. When I went back into the house I was so drunk that I couldn't find the guest bedroom and went instead into the master bedroom where I tried to get in bed with the sleeping Carol. Rupe caught me just in time and carried me into the other room.

For my 70th birthday tribute Carol wrote:

"Hello John. I remember the time you spent the night prior to a fishing trip with Rupert. After several drinks, you attempted to get into the sack with me but Rupert redirected you to the spare bedroom. So sorry. It would have been the time of your life. Have a great birthday!

You are a wonderful friend. Thanks for the memories. Carol Hess."

The next morning Rupe woke me up at 4a.m. for our drive to the Bay Area. Luckily, one of his neighbors drove us to the boat as neither Rupe nor I were in any condition to do any driving. Once we were out to sea, one of the crew members gave me a fishing pole, baited it, cast the line out, and placed it in a holder attached to the deck. I guess I was fishing. The rest of the day floated by on vast amounts of beer and the telling of off-color stories. In the afternoon my fishing line started to bob and a crew member hauled in a fish that he claimed was not a "keeper", so he threw it back out to sea, thank God! The day finally ended, and on my drive home I vowed that this would be my first and last fishing trip.

I worked for Telos for slightly over thirteen years and with the exception of the last couple of years it was a thoroughly enjoyable experience. One of the factors in making it so pleasant was my boss, Dick Brewer, the president of our division. His philosophy was that if you were not having fun with what you were doing, maybe you should be doing something else. Whenever we had a regional managers meeting, whoever put the agenda together had better include fun as one of the agenda items. When any of us managers hit a roadblock in our pursuit of business, Dick would pull out one of his favorite expressions, "It's going to be okay." He would then work with us till we found a solution for whatever problem we were facing

My Sacramento region was profitable from day one and would remain so for my entire career with Telos. At the end of my first year, I had ten Telosians working for me, which was exactly what my business plan called for. Dick flew up to Sacramento and took Bobbie and me out for dinner at the Bullmarket Restaurant in order to celebrate my first anniversary with the company. Sometime during the course of the meal, Dick slipped me a piece of paper that said that my salary was immediately increased by $12,000.00 to $60,000.00 per year. I almost fell off my chair and couldn't wait to get in the car with Bobbie so I could share the good news with her.

Dick had another expression that he used with a great deal of frequency. One time Bobbie and I took him to a King's basketball game. The Kings, who were really a lousy team at that time, were playing the Lakers and were being thoroughly trashed. Dick, the consummate Laker's fan, turned to Bobbie and me and said, "It don't get any better than this." He really enjoyed life, and you knew he was having a good time when this phrase popped out.

After about a year or so, I moved out of Bob's office and into Suite 310, taking Kate with me. Rather than have Kate sit out front, I had her desk put in my office. This was so she could listen to my phone conversations and watch me while I interviewed candidates for whatever openings that I had at the time. I also took Kate on sales calls with me so she could learn how I presented Telos's capabilities to my clients. This is the technique that I employed for mentoring employees and for preparing them for higher positions in the organization, and it worked.

The State of California had a very cumbersome procedure for obtaining technical talent. When a State department needed some temporary technical help they would issue an R.F.P. (A Request for Proposal). They would send the R.F.P. to the companies that provided this type of service and the companies would in turn deliver a proposal to the department that made the request. An evaluation would take place and finally an award would be made to the company that had the best response. This process would take several months and would delay whatever it was that the department wanted to accomplish.

It was my opinion that the State would be better served (and so would Telos) if the State had a list of pre-approved vendors that they could just call on without having to go through this lengthy procurement process. I had a lot of friends at the various State agencies who liked my concept and they formed a technical committee that worked behind the scenes to have this concept adopted. Finally, about a year later the Department of General Services issued an R.F.P. for the establishment of a "Master Services Agreement for Technical Services." Naturally, Telos submitted a winning proposal that opened the door to tons of State business. At one point, we had almost 100 technical staff working for the various State departments. Every time the State would rebid this contract, I would win. I consider having the great State of California implement my concept as one of my crowning achievements in a very long career.

Another one of my special clients was the Department of Information Technology for the City of Sacramento, managed by my good friend, Jim Puthuff. Jim, and his wife Barbara, organized a trail ride for members of his department and invited Bobbie and me to join them. I put horseback riding right up there with fishing when it comes to things that I like to do. However, it was another opportunity for me to socialize with my client so I accepted the invitation, never having been on a horse before.

In order to prepare for this event, Bobbie and I signed up for a horseback-riding lesson. Bobbie actually did not need the lesson as she had ridden horses years before, but I certainly did. We took our one lesson, and now I was thoroughly prepared for the trail ride.

When we arrived at the stable the ranch hand asked me if I had ever ridden before. "Many times," I lied. He introduced me to my horse, Molly, and helped me mount her. The trail ride took a couple of hours and was rather pleasant because our horses all kept to a leisurely pace. Once at the campground that was our destination, there was a nice spread of food and lots of beer and soft drinks for everyone.

The ride back to the stable was a nightmare. Molly wanted to get back to her barn as soon as possible and no amount of tugging on her reins slowed her down. I, unfortunately, had drunk more than my fair share of beer, and with Molly running uncontrollably, I thought my bladder was going to burst before I got back to the stable. Plus, a lot of the more experienced riders had gotten quite drunk and were causing the novices to fall off their horses. I hung on for dear life as I was determined not to pee in my pants and embarrass myself. We finally made it back and I added horseback riding, right along with fishing, as something to do once, but never again!

My oldest daughter, Ann, was living up at Lake Tahoe, working as a Keno runner. I loved to bet on football games and since Ann worked in a casino, she would place the bets for me. I liked to bet on a three-team parlay that paid 6 1/2 to one if you were successful. I gave Ann $20.00 at the beginning of the season and by the time the play-offs were at hand I had over $1,000.00 to collect from Ann. Bobbie and I made arrangements to meet Ann at one of the swanky casino restaurants for a celebratory dinner. When she arrived at the restaurant she said:

"Dad, I've got some good news and some bad news for you. Which do you want to hear first?"

"I guess I'd rather hear the good news first," I replied.

"I collected $1,130.00 for your bets this season."

"Wonderful", I said. "Now what's the bad news?"

"I was arrested today and my bail was set at $1,100.00 and I had to use your winnings to get out of jail, so here's your $30.00."

The dinner for the three of us came to about $30.00 so I wound up the season with nothing. Ann had some outstanding warrants for her arrest for not paying speeding tickets and when she was stopped for having a broken tail light, she was arrested on those old warrants. Oh well!

At the beginning of each football season, I would place a $100.00 bet that the 49ers would win the Super Bowl. The only season that I neglected to place this bet was the 1981 season when they won their first Super Bowl. The odds that year were 100 to 1, so I lost out on cashing in $10,000.00. They won their 3rd Super Bowl in the 1988 season. That was the year that Bobbie and I were lucky enough to win the lottery for tickets to the game that would take took place in Florida, and we decided to go. Raymond Valdes was living in Miami at that time and he offered us the use of his condominium for our stay.

Shortly after moving to El Dorado Hills, Susan and Raymond got married. Because both of them had been married before, they had a small ceremony in their home with family and a few close friends in attendance. They probably would have been better off just living together without being married. It didn't take too long before things started to fall apart and Susan bought back her original unit at the Bluffs and has been living there ever since they were divorced.

Raymond picked us up at the airport in Miami and drove us to his condo in Biscayne Bay. It was an elegant unit, furnished in a classy and expensive style. During our stay, Raymond moved in with his girlfriend, a beautiful and sexy lady from Columbia whose father owned the main Columbia Airline. Raymond leased both a Rolls Royce and Mercedes sedan and offered us the use of either car during our visit. Raymond was in the chips again either through an infusion of cash from his family or as a result of the success of his new business venture. He was importing fish from Chile and selling them to the local markets and restaurants in Florida. His luxurious lifestyle led me to believe that these fish must have had a little white powder tucked away in their bellies.

I chose the Mercedes and the first day I drove it, the temperature was about 95 degrees. I turned on what I thought was the air conditioner but instead was the heater. I didn't know how to shut the damn thing off and Bobbie and I were soaking wet before we found a gas station mechanic who fixed the problem for us. I have never been fond of Mercedes cars since that event.

On the Saturday evening, before the Super Bowl, in order to thank Raymond for his wonderful hospitality, I invited him and his girlfriend out for dinner at a restaurant of his choice. What a mistake! The food, drinks, wine, company and ambiance were marvelous but I could have stayed at a five-star hotel for what that meal cost me. Raymond being Raymond thought it was quite amusing when I almost choked on being presented the bill.

The next day we went to the Super Bowl and since the 49ers won, I won my preseason bet and had $1,000.00 waiting for mc to collect at South Lake Tahoe. This time Ann was not involved in the collection process. Raymond also taped the game for us and after all these years, I still have it.

When I was in my late thirties, I started to lose my hair and was rapidly balding. When I turned forty, I decided to treat myself to a toupee, and I have worn hairpieces on and off ever since. One time, while I was working for B.R.I., I had to travel to Springfield, Illinois, where we maintained an office. To get there, I had to travel to and change planes in Chicago. The small plane to Springfield left from the tarmac, since there was no Jetway available for boarding. As I approached the plane, carrying a suitcase in one hand and a briefcase in the other, a strong gust of wind started to lift the toupee off my head. A stewardess, standing on the top step of the plane, saw what was happening, raced down the stairs, and put her hand on top of my head while I climbed the stairs. She saved me about $1,500.00 and created a great deal of laughter and merriment for my fellow passengers.

Another time, Judi Gesh, my Reno office manager for Telos, and I were marketing in Boise, Idaho. We got out to the client site and got hit by a wind and rainstorm. For my 70th birthday tribute Judi wrote:

"...After running into the building, I turned and asked John how bad my hair looked. His response to me was, 'To hell with yours, what is mine doing? Is it still on?' We both started laughing hysterically.

"After regaining our composure we went into the meeting. When we greeted the client he made the statement, 'Gee, John, you look great but different. You seem taller!!!' Needless to say all during our meeting while looking at John's head I tried not to laugh."

One of the traditions I established while working for Telos was an annual football party at one of the casino hotels in Reno. I would invite several clients and some of my key managers and we would party and watch football, preferably a 49ers game. Art Rankin, who once worked for me and then worked for Sacramento County as a client of mine wrote:

"John, its about *the hair*. There have been so many laughs. I especially remember the time you came into Jamie's for lunch so pissed off that smoke was coming out of your ears. You ordered a Bloody Mary, then announced that you were planning to kill your barber – the SOB had cut *the hair*.

"Then there was the time we were in Reno for a football party. We all gambled, drank, and played half the night. Needless to say we felt no pain by the time we stumbled to our rooms. The next morning I complemented you on your new hat. Your reply was, 'Art, I lost the damn toupee.' You decided that it must be somewhere in the casino and were trying to find out how you could get security to discreetly search for it. Of course, it turned up in a dresser drawer."

Several years later, I was invited to a blackjack tournament at the Atlantis Casino, in Reno. I came in 33rd out of a field of 240 and actually won $100.00. More importantly, I stayed up until the wee hours of the morning drinking and gambling and having a lot of fun. The next morning, while I was still in a fog, Bobbie and I packed up for the short trip back home to Carson City. When I unpacked my bag, I discovered that my toupee was missing and, before I panicked, I called the Atlantis Lost and Found department to find out if anyone had turned in a hairpiece. The nice lady said that no toupees had been turned in but that she would check with the maid responsible for cleaning my room and call me back if she had any luck. Several hours later I received a call from her telling me that the "item" that I had mentioned to her had been found and she would be happy to mail it to me. I swore that that would be the last time I would wear the damn thing in a casino again!

Up until 1986, Kate and I were the only office staff that Telos had in Sacramento. I decided that I wanted to venture out into the permanent placement field as well as continuing with the information technology staffing business. Dick was not very supportive of this concept, nor were my fellow regional managers. They felt it was counterproductive to our main line of business. Anyway, I persuaded Dick to let me try and so I hired Marty Maskall to be the manager of my Permanent Placement Division. I knew Marty for a few years while she was working for Management Recruiters. Marty and I had done several deals together that were mutually profitable.

Marty was very successful in the four years that she worked for me and produced a lot of revenue and profit for Telos. In 1990 she decided to leave Telos in order to publish her book, *The Attitude Treasury: 101 inspiring quotations*. I was sorry to see her go but I kept in touch with her over the years, and was able to rehire her in 1999 when I was working for Pilot Computer Services.

The next expansion move that I made was to get into government consulting. To that end, I hired my old buddy, Neal X. Jones. I first hired Neal while we were having a couple of martinis at the University Club. I immediately sent him up to a client of mine in Olympia, Washington for which he has never forgiven me. That was back in the old B.R.I. days. After B.R.I. collapsed, Neal and Bob Hansen took over what was left of my old Transportation Division and grew the business to the point where they were able to sell it to Grant Thornton, a large C.P.A. firm. After the sale, Neal struck out on his own, operating Neal Jones and Associates. Although he was quite successful on his own, he was attracted to what I could offer him at Telos. Once again, Dick was not wildly enthusiastic about my plan, but he did allow me to hire Neal

Neal wrote,

"I had no sooner met John when he offered me a job with a new company that he and Aaron were forming. I, of course, was flattered that so august a person as John would present such an offer. (It later turned out that they desperately needed someone to go to Olympia, Washington to manage a contract because the current person was sick of being there.) I accepted and the adventure began which led me to my current state of ruin.

"Once I was in his clutches, John took me to Olympia where he introduced me to his clients. The Secretary of Institutions and the psychologist in charge of research (one Dr. Holiday…a prophetic name which still brings a chill to my heart after all these many years.)

"John took me up there, introduced me to the client, and left me. For the next two years I would contact John by phone or by flying down to L.A. or Sacramento. (It was made clear that many calls were frowned upon.) During our infrequent chats by phone, I would ask when he would be coming to the Northwest. The reply was always the same, "Soon." The situation continued for two years and he never came to Olympia again. "Soon" was the code name used to mean, "When pigs fly."

One of the first assignments that I got for Neal was a part-time study of a case tracking system used by the Sacramento County's District Attorney's office. Neal, the consummate consultant, developed this project from a part-time study to a full-blown development effort. Not only did Telos develop a new system for the DA, but we also received a contract to run the system for them. I recently asked Jerry Kincaid, a fellow that had worked for me at B.R.I. and who Neal had hired to be the chief architect of the new system, what the current status of the system was.

I sent Jerry the following:

"Since I am not able to work, I have been writing my autobiography. I am at the point in the story where I had Russ Waltrip hire Neal Jones to do some part-time consulting at the DA's office. That was the origin of the CRIMES system."Can you tell me what CRIMES stands for, to what organizations you have sold it, and how many millions of dollars in revenue it has produced?

"I promise to treat you kindly in my book!" His response was: "CRIMES stands for Criminal Records Information Management and Exchange System. The "Criminal Records Information Management" portion of the title refers to the collecting and updating of data necessary to automate the workflow of Prosecuting Attorney and Public Defender offices.

The "Exchange" portion of the title refers to interfaces and integration elements that facilitate the flow of information amongst the various member agencies of the Law and Justice community. For example, we interface with court systems to send information about new cases which the district attorney has decided to prosecute, and to receive information about the court's docket – hearing date, judge assigned, and outcome.

"We have installed and continue to provide annual support for CRIMES in 12 6 offices from coast to coast – from Portland, Maine to Portland, Oregon. Our largest clients include Sacramento, Santa Clara County, the afore-mentioned Portland, OR (Multnomah County, Cook County (Chicago), the State of Louisiana, and the State of Alaska. Our revenue to date is $19M, including software sales, customization services, and continuing support.

"It's a nice story, isn't it?"

In 1987, Kate's husband, Preston, found out that the company that he worked for was leaving Sacramento for Santa Cruz. This was a sad time for me because Kate and I had grown incredibly close and having her leave Telos was like losing my right arm. However, life goes on and I needed to find a replacement for Kate. I contacted Judy, who had worked for Jay and me when I worked for Boeing Computer Services. She indicated that she might be available.

The day after I contacted Judy, I had lunch with Harold (Flash) and Melissa Flaspohler. Flash had worked for me on a variety of assignments since I started the Sacramento office for Telos. Bobbie and I had gotten friendly with them as a couple and had a lot of fun with them over drinks and dinner on many occasions. At lunch, I explained to them that I needed to find someone to replace Kate and I was thinking about hiring my old secretary from Boeing. Melissa's response was, "What about me?"

Melissa had just gotten her Masters degree in Business Administration from Sacramento State University and was looking for a job. We agreed that I would interview her the following day in my office. Despite the fact that we were friends, I conducted a formal interview in order to satisfy myself that she would be an adequate substitute for Kate. At the conclusion of the interview, Melissa said, "Now, can we go out and have a drink?" That did it. I was going to offer her the job.

Melissa worked for me from 1987 until I left Telos in 1995. I taught and mentored Melissa over the years, and she progressed from being my assistant to becoming the Sacramento Regional Manager. I promoted her to vice-president before I left. Melissa and Flash are still good friends and Bobbie and I visit with them several times a year.

When I first started working for Dick, Telos Consulting Services had six offices, Boston, Fullerton, Los Angeles, Santa Barbara, Santa Clara and Seattle. Sacramento was unique in that it was the only regional office to pursue government and business application programming. All the other offices concentrated on scientific and real-time systems. One of the truly great things about working for T.C.S. was that there was no corporate bullshit to contend with. Each manager ran his or her operation as if it was our own enterprise, and no two of us were alike in how we conducted business. Corporate provided the accounting and personnel functions and were there totally for our support. They did not try to act as controlling organizations like some other companies that I have worked for. It was this entrepreneurial atmosphere that Dick promoted which led to the success of his division.

We would have regional manager's meetings once or twice a year. These were very spirited events that took place in the various locations where we had offices. Each of the managers, me included, had huge egos, and we were all positive that we knew the right way to grow the business. Since there was no "one right way", our meetings seemed more like barroom brawls than civilized discussions. Since we respected and trusted one another, when we went our separate ways, there were no long lasting hard feelings that I was aware of. Dick would frequently end the meeting by saying, "It's going to be alright!"

I wanted to expand my region into the State of Nevada. I liked Carson City, the capital of Nevada, and always enjoyed doing business there since my early days working for Aerojet. The MIS Director for the State at that time, 1988, was Hale Bennett. Although I made several appointment to meet with Hale, every time I arrived at his office he was either at a meeting or was unavailable for me, and I would be shuffled off to one of his subordinates. I found out that there was a fellow who had just quit working for Hale that might be the right guy to help me break the ice with the director. That's how I got to meet Sid Gesh, an ex-Navy Commander, and now an ex-Nevada State employee. After several meetings with Sid, he agreed to come to work for me with the goal of selling Hale on the establishment of a Master Services Agreement similar to the one I had with the State of California.

Sid arranged a meeting for me with Hale and we both presented this concept to him. He seemed very receptive to the idea. Like always, I made Hale, my potential client, my friend, and got to meet his lovely wife, Kay who was a Supervisor for Carson City. Sid, his wife Judi, Bobbie and I would occasionally have dinner with Hale and Kay and mutual trust and respect was established. It took about a year until Telos was awarded a sole source Master Services Contract to provide system analysts and programmers to the State of Nevada.

Sid and I thought that Las Vegas would be a natural market place for Telos in addition to Carson City. We decided to make a call on the MIS Director for Clark County. His office was in the County Courthouse building. We noticed that there was a long line of people waiting to get into the courthouse. Since the U.S. was fully involved in the first Gulf War at that time, we though nothing of it and got at the end of the line, assuming that we had to pass through a metal detector before being admitted into the building.

As we approached the head of the stairs, we noticed that people were looking at us and giggling. What we hadn't realized was that it was Valentine's Day, and the line we were standing in was for the marriage license office. We had a good laugh and went on to our meeting. That night over dinner, Sid gave me a plastic wedding band that he bought in the gift shop at the hotel where we were staying. We've had a lot of fun with that event over the years. Sid wrote,

"We exchanged flowers and candy on our anniversary for many years. One year, John presented me with a pair of the ugliest cufflinks you have ever seen. It happened that when John and Barbara were on a business trip in Boise, John forgot his cufflinks. Barbara, being the thoughtful person she is, went out and picked up an inexpensive pair for him to use. John didn't have the heart to tell her how much he hated those things, so he gave them to his 'significant other'.

"Not too long after I received the cufflinks, I mentioned to John that he was responsible for paying one half of our 'son's' (Tim) tuition to Notre Dame. John choked and refused. I immediately contacted my lawyer and had him draw up divorce papers on the basis of child abandonment. John was really surprised when he was served with the divorce papers. John went on to prepare a counter suit claiming that I was an unfit parent. So we ended our marriage."

After we were awarded the Master Service Contract, I appointed Judi Gesh as my manager of the Nevada region for Telos. Sid, bless his heart, is a wonderful consultant and project leader but he will be the first to admit that he is not a salesman. Judi, over the years, not only built the State practice but also developed many clients in both the public and private sectors in Reno as well as Las Vegas. She always did an outstanding job and was still working for me at MSXI when I was terminated at the end of 2002. Sid assisted Judi in writing many winning proposals and served as a project manager on many of them. Sid and Judi are among our closest friends.

One spring day, Al Ortiz invited Bobbie and me to spend a weekend camping with him and his wife, Alice. I had known Al since the Aerojet days and we were good friends with him and Alice. Al was one of Jim Puthuff's managers at the City of Sacramento. Although I swore that I would never sleep in a tent again after getting out of the service, I viewed this as a marketing opportunity as Al was a client as well as a friend.

We drove up to a campsite near Bodega Bay and Al proceeded to set up the tent that was mounted on his trailer. We were located about 200 yards from the bathroom and shower area. As night fell we had several cocktails and Al started a fire both for warmth and to be used for cooking our dinner. It became bitterly cold so we huddled as close to the fire as possible in an attempt to keep warm. Bobbie was wearing sneakers and had one foot on a rock right close to the fire. The sole of the sneaker melted and adhered to the rock; we might have found that funny if we weren't so damn cold. When Bobbie tried to stand, she twisted her ankle because of the rock, and almost fell into the campfire.

After dinner, we crawled into the tent in an attempt to sleep. Al had some kind of heater going but I hadn't been this cold since my days in Korea. Around midnight I had the urge to pee so I took my flashlight and followed the path to the urinals. Bu the time I got there, I couldn't perform because I was frozen solid. The next morning after taking showers in the filthiest bathroom I had ever seen, I told Al and Alice that I would treat them to dinner if we could break camp and get back to civilization. Camping is right up there with fishing and horseback riding on my "not to do" list.

As the 1980's wore on, Telos Consulting Services enjoyed great success and expanded into new territories. We opened offices in Washington, D.C., Austin and Houston, Texas, and Atlanta, Georgia. Dick promoted me, Pat Bailey, (Regional Manager of Santa Clara), and Bruce Eckhoff, (Regional Manager of Fullerton) to the positions of vice president with responsibility for several regions. I, in turn, promoted Melissa Flaspohler to my old job as regional manager of the Sacramento office. She did an outstanding job for Telos and continued doing so even after I left the company in 1995.

Of the many things that I learned over my years of managing

salespeople, one was to be suspicious of lists of overly optimistic reports of sales opportunities that keep growing. I inherited the Atlanta Region and Ron, its regional manager. I should have been wary of Ron the first time I met him. I flew east to meet him and he and his wife took me to probably the most expensive restaurant in Atlanta, the Abbey. Ron was extremely handsome, articulate, and charming, as was his wife. We had a lovely dinner and since Ron paid for it, I had no idea how much it cost until he sent me his expense report for approval. Yikes!!

The next morning, I met with Ron in his office and we reviewed a rather extensive list of sales opportunities that he was exploring. To say the least, I was impressed and believed I had a winner in Ron. As time went on, Ron's list got larger and larger but there were no sales happening and that made me nervous. I decided to visit Ron again and when I got to Atlanta I asked him if we could make a joint sales call on his hottest prospect. Well, we made a sales call all right, except that Ron did not know where his best prospect was located and took me to the wrong building. It quickly became apparent that his sales prospects were bogus and that in reality he was not what one might call a legitimate type of guy.

For me, one of the hardest tasks as a manager or executive is having to fire someone. Even if I know it is the absolutely right thing to do, I lose sleep and agonize over my decision. It was especially so in Ron's case. He certainly had all the tools to make a great salesman but he was lacking in the one trait that I demand of all my employees, integrity. If I can't trust someone, no matter what his or her other characteristics might be, that individual will have to work elsewhere. And so it was with Ron. Subsequent examinations of his expense reports and other data proved that I had made the right decision.

Telos Corporation, in addition to having the Consulting Division, also had two other divisions, Field Engineering and the Federal Systems Divisions. The CEO of Telos, Lin Conger, was also one of the founders of the company. Telos is a Greek word that means "tending toward an end." Additional meanings are, "completion of a cycle, consummation, perfection, end result."

After running the company for so many years, Lin wanted to cash out, and to that end Telos went public in 1990. This was the beginning of the end of good times at Telos. As a publicly traded company, listed on the Nasdaq exchange, there were a lot more financial controls required for the benefit of the shareholders, and fun was now no longer an agenda item. Dick left the company at the end of 1990 and Phil Schaefer, Lin's replacement, appointed me, Pat, and Bruce to run T.C.S. as a troika. Although, the three of us rarely agreed on anything, it was a smart decision on Phil's part because we balanced each other out and our division had continued success. However, more changes were on the way.

In 1991 Contel bought Telos. It was a stock purchase so all the stockholders got paid for their shares by Contel. This meant that Lin and several other early Telos employees became overnight millionaires. Although I joined Telos late in the game I still had some stock for which Contel paid me $80,000.00. Contel did not make any management changes and we pretty much ran the company like we had in the past. The next change occurred when G.T.E bought Contel. What G.T.E. had not realized that there was a conflict of interest in the work the Telos and G.T.E did for the same client, the Department of Defense. The Department of Defense told G.T.E. that they would have to sell Telos or they would be forced to cancel millions of dollars worth of business that G.T.E. had with them. G.T.E. put Telos in a blind trust till they could find a buyer.

Once again, there were no management changes and we continued to prosper. There was one really beneficial event that occurred because of G.T.E.'s ownership of us. G.T.E. had a policy, unlike Telos, that if an employee was laid off he was entitled to severance pay, the amount of which was dependent on his length of service. The minimum amount was three months.

Hale Bennett wanted to open an office in Las Vegas and asked us to find him a communications engineer to staff it for him. Not knowing that the Nevada legislature had specifically forbidden Hale from opening a southern office, we complied and found him a very capable individual that we hired and contracted to Hale's department.

When the legislature found out about this and the fact that Hale had given Telos a sole source contract, the shit hit the fan, and Hale was fired and replaced by Karen Kavenaugh who immediately canceled our contract with the State. We had thirteen employees working for the State and the G.T.E. severance package was a Godsend since they would get paid while we were looking for other assignments for them. The employee in Las Vegas had only been with us a few weeks but he got three months pay because of G.T.E.'s policy. It took Judi and I over six months to win Karen over and get back our contract with the State. This time, however, it was not a sole source contract. Several other vendors were awarded contracts after responding to a R.F.P. that Karen's department issued.

Towards the end of 1993 G.T.E. sold Telos to a company with the strange name of C-3, whose business was manufacturing computers that were impervious to the weather and selling them to the military. At that time, I was responsible for Sacramento, Nevada, Seattle, Atlanta, Colorado Springs, Government Consulting, and a new division, Systems Integration.

When I first got to meet my new leaders, I knew I was in a heap of trouble. The CEO, John, and one of his key lieutenants, Joe, were Wall Street guys, in their early thirties. They were full of themselves and were going to show us how to run our business.

At dinner that night, Joe, who was sitting next to me said,

"John, I understand that that CRIMES package that you guys developed in Sacramento is terrific and I'm going to tell you how to sell it. What you need to do is hire a whole bunch of commission salesmen, and have them sell to the government agencies that need this system. You flood the market with this system, all at the same time."

"Joe," I responded. "What a good idea. Let me talk it over with Neal Jones and have him implement your suggestion." What I thought was, *You stupid schmuck, you have no concept of how the government works and your idea is the stupidest thing I have ever heard.*

The management of C-3 was enamored with T.Q.M. (Total Quality

Management) and spent thousands of dollars sending staff to seminars and training classes. T.Q.M. is a management technique developed by the Japanese to improve the quality of the products that they manufactured. It is a system widely used in this country by manufacturing companies as well. The C-3 management wanted to impose this methodology on Telos, which I vigorously opposed, and that was the start of many battles that I would have with John and company. I didn't see how a methodology designed to improve the quality of products could be meaningful in a consulting environment. Also, I had been subject to many management methodologies over my career such as M.O.B. (Management by Objectives), P.E.R.T., etc. etc. None of them substituted for good common sense, integrity, honesty, and hard work.

Soon after the acquisition of Telos, John decided that what was not broken needed fixing. To that end he decided to appoint Keith as President of Telos Consulting Services, and Pat, Bruce, and I now reported to Keith. Keith had been a manager of the Telos Federal System's Division, and didn't have a clue as to what we were all about. At first I liked Keith, but Bobbie, after having lunch with the two of us, told me to watch out as she sensed something devious about him.

After a few months, Keith decided to make Sacramento the headquarters for his division. I think he made this decision because I had hired Jan Cooper to work for Telos after she had been let go by Blue Diamond. I think he was attracted to her and thought perhaps he could establish a relationship with her. At any rate, Sacramento became his home office, and since I did not have any office space available for him, Keith took over my office and now I had to work from home.

In the grand tradition of fixing things that were not broken established by John, Keith, at a management meeting that took place in Santa Clara, proposed an organizational change whereby I would turn over all my organizations to Pat, and my assignment would be to travel full time attempting to get contracts with other States across the nation.

I told Keith that this was a harebrained idea, and I was willing to travel 50 percent of my time, but I was not about to relinquish control of the organizations I had worked so hard to establish. Keith backed down from this reorganization plan but from that day forward it became apparent that he was out to get me. The situation came to a head at the end of 1993 when John invited Pat and Bruce back to corporate headquarters to meet with him and Keith, with instructions for Pat and Bruce not to let me know of this meeting. Of course, they told me about this. The purpose of the meeting was to break up my organization and demote me. Keith's backstabbing almost worked. When I got wind of what happened I sent the following letter to John:

November 17, 1993

Dear John:

When you receive this letter I don't want you to have the perception that I am mad, I am damn mad.

I think it was unconscionable of you and Keith to invite my fellow vice-presidents back to corporate to discuss their future roles within the organization and instruct them not to let me know. It was reprehensible of you to present a reorganization plan to my peers, whereby you suggested breaking up my organization and demoting me, without giving me the opportunity to present the facts — as opposed to accepting Keith's lies and distortions about my work habits and initiative.

I find it peculiar that after almost a two-year involvement with Telos, you told Pat and Bruce that you did not know anything about me except what Keith told you.

Just to recap, I have been with Telos for almost twelve years. I started the business in Sacramento and grew it to its current position of eminence. I have worked nights, weekends, holidays, and long days for Telos since I started, and have never taken a sick day in those twelve years. To say I work six-hour days is a bold-faced lie and probably is a result of when Keith was in Sacramento and took the only available office. Having no spare space, I had to establish an office in my home. When I went into the Sacramento office I had no desk and would obviously come in late and leave early in order to accomplish my work at home. If Keith had a problem with my work habits he should have confronted me; however, he never did, and told a falsehood to you.

As for refusing to travel, that is another bald-faced lie. At our Santa Clara meeting Keith suggested that I turn my operation over to Pat and travel to other states for new business purposes. I said I thought this was an absurd idea, but I was willing to travel 50 percent of my time to accomplish his objectives. Pat and Bruce were witnesses to this conversation. In addition, when Keith assigned Seattle and Atlanta to me, I frequently traveled and took the necessary action that Keith was too cowardly to accomplish. I have never objected to necessary travel.

As far as retirement is concerned, I repeatedly told Keith that I planned to work until I was 92 because I have no hobbies and all I know how to do is work. Ask any member of my staff about this.

At this stage of my life and with all the effort I have put in on behalf of Telos, I am deeply wounded that you would want to demote me and carve up the organization that I have worked so diligently to create, based on the lies of a man desperately trying to cling to his job.

Far be it from me to tell you what to do, but if I had an employee who lied to me and stabbed one of his trusting subordinates in the back, I think I know what action I would take.

I don't know how we will recover from this situation, but I want you to know that I am deeply upset and angry over these events.

John K. Silberman
Vice President
Government Systems Group

This truly was the beginning of the end for me. Although John reassigned Keith to another position in the company, and reestablished the troika to run T.C.S., I could no longer trust John, and knew my days were numbered. The three of us found out that John had given Keith a $20,000.00 bonus for screwing up our division and that certainly didn't sit well with us.

I had one more triumph left in me before I was forced to resign. Judi and I had spent some time in Boise, Idaho, marketing our services. When we met with some success by placing a few people at the State, I decided to open an office in downtown Boise. I hired Ron Pharis to be the manager reporting to Judi Gesh. This was shortly before I left Telos and Ron and his wife Florence, flourished in that market place.

Before I left, the troika decided, and rightfully so, that one of us should be appointed president of the division before John had a chance to send another Keith to lead us. Pat didn't want the job, and I knew I would never be able to work with John, so Bruce was the logical choice. Bruce became president and did an excellent job, both before and after I left.

John kept harassing me. I needed to move the Sacramento operation to new offices. There were 15 staffers working in a space designed for 11. John refused to approve the move, although, right after I left, he moved the Sacramento office into far more expensive digs than what I planned. He criticized my handwriting, telling me that I should have someone else prepare my expense reports. My handwriting has been bad my entire life, but I never had a boss call me on it. I had planned a trip to Paris to attend a conference with Neal and he wouldn't let me go until Bruce intervened. Telos got a ton of business as a result of that meeting in Paris. And so it went. Finally, I made a decision and sent the following e-mail to Bruce and Pat on February 27, 1995:

"After spending an agonizing weekend, considering all the factors, I have come to a decision....

This is a sad day for me because I have loved Telos as much as a man can love a company. It is unfortunate that the management changes that have occurred over the past few years have forced me to consider leaving before I was ready to, and before I wanted to. It appears that the current management wants me out because of their perception that my age is detrimental to their future plans.

Please indulge an 'old man' to boast about his accomplishments for the company over the past 13 years. I am proud that I started the Sacramento office and grew it to its position of prominence within the community and within our division. I am proud that I taught Melissa the business and trained her to become a highly effective manager. I am proud that I started the Reno office and trained Judi to be a wonderful manager. I am proud that I could persuade a senior nationally known expert like Neal to join Telos. I am proud of hiring Paul to lead my integration group. I am proud of my initiative to open the Boise office….

I am proud that I have won every re-bid for the County of Sacramento and the State of California over the course of my career with Telos. I am proud of making money for the company each and every year that I have been employed by Telos. I am proud of the hundreds of jobs that I created and the hundreds of employees for whom I created employment.

So you see I am offering to leave with my head held high and with the dignity and respect that I deserve…."

It took me about a month to negotiate what I thought was a reasonably fair severance package. I resigned effective March 31, 1995 and sent the following e-mail to the many friends and associates that I had within Telos:

"To those of you who know me, you realize what Telos has meant to me. To me, Telos was more than a company, it was a way of life. Things change, and to each of you Telosians with whom I've shared a life, laugh, a drink, a triumph, a friendship, I bid you adieu."

And so that chapter in my life ended, as did this chapter in my book.

Chapter Eleven
Pilot Computer Services

1995 - 1999

"Jewish people are not drinkers," my mother used to say. "Except for maybe a little Manschewitz wine on Passover." If this broad generalization has any truth to it, I am the glaring exception to that rule. Ever since polishing off a pint of Philadelphia whiskey with Dick Kessler when I was fourteen years old, I have been, what people might consider to be a moderate to heavy drinker. So after leaving Telos, when one of my buddies, Russ Farr, suggested that we look into buying a bar, I was game for it.

I had known Russ for a number of years as an employee, client, and friend. He knew the owner of an old established bar and restaurant who was looking to sell. Russ and his dad, Sidney, Frankie Lopez, Bobbie and I formed an unequal partnership and purchased Ernie's for $50,000.00. Bobbie and I owned 20 percent as did Frankie, and Russ and his dad owned the other 60 percent. The place was filthy when we bought it and we spent a couple of months cleaning it up, buying new kitchen equipment, and generally redoing the joint. We decided to reopen as a sports bar and named it "The Player's Lounge."

Bobbie spent many hours making covers for the bar stools and curtains for the windows that separated the bar from the dining area. She used material that contained the logos of the various NFL teams and when we opened the place for business it looked terrific. After being open for a few weeks, it appeared that the business was running smoothly so Bobbie and I took our annual vacation to Puerto Vallarta, Mexico. When we returned, I discovered that all was not well with "The Player's Lounge". Checks had been written without the amounts being recorded in the check register, little IOU slips of paper were all over the place, inventory control had not been established, and for the number of bottles of liquor consumed there seemed to be a surprising lack of cash in the nightly deposits.

Russ had a full-time job working for the State, and Frankie also worked full time for SMUD, our local utility district. Since I was the only one with time on my hands, it became my responsibility to establish the controls that a cash business like a bar and restaurant required, which I did. In order to be successful in this type of business, one of the owners must be present most of the time because no matter how many controls are established, in the absence of the owners, the bartenders and other employees will figure ways to cheat. So, I had a choice to make. Did I want to spend the next several years running this type of business or not? The answer came quickly and easily. I certainly enjoyed being on the side of the bar that had the stools but did not enjoy being on the other side. I left the management of the place to the manager that Russ had hired and reverted to the status of an investor, of a rather poor investment, as it worked out. After five years, the place closed down, and I did not receive even a one penny return on my investment. When Russ sold off the assets, Bobbie and I did get a few thousand dollars of our original investment back. I really don't think the place was a failure, I just think we got screwed over. But life goes on.

On one of our trips to Carson City, when I was still working for Telos, Bobbie and I bought some property in Silver Springs. Silver Springs is a tiny town about 30 miles east of Carson City. We bought 10 acres of raw land that could be subdivided into two five-acre parcels. We also bought another five-acre parcel that had a brand new manufactured home on it. Our thinking was that we could develop the two five-acre parcels and they would provide some income while we lived in the manufactured house. In the meanwhile we would rent out the house until such time as we wanted it for ourselves.

Since I was no longer working and was not interested in running the bar, Bobbie and I thought that the time had come for us to move to Nevada and begin life as a retired couple in Silver Springs. All of our friends thought we were nuts; the town had nothing to offer but one little casino, bar and restaurant, and didn't even have a library or movie theatre. We were determined to make this move until I had lunch one day with Peter Jackson, one of the three founders of Pilot Computer Services. I had used Pilot as one of my subcontractors to fulfill the minority requirements that the State and County imposed on their prime vendors. We had to subcontract 15 percent of our awards to a minority owned firm, which Pilot was, in order to comply with the law.

When I told Peter what my plans were he told me that Pilot had been awarded a contract with the State of Nevada similar to the contract that Telos had enjoyed. He said that he went to Carson City every few weeks to market their contract, but since I would be living close by, "Would you be interested in doing some part-time work for Pilot?"

I leaped at the opportunity, because the prospect of not working was very frightening to me, and on August 25, 1995, I signed a marketing contract with Pilot Computer Services. For $900.00 a month, I would be their guy in Carson City selling to the State. ($900.00 per month was the same salary that I received when I started with Aerojet in 1961).

Having made this decision impacted where Bobbie and I would live. We could have moved to Silver Springs like we had originally planned but we decided that living in Carson City would be better because all the State offices were located there. Although Silver Springs was only forty minutes away, the thought of driving that distance twice a day was not appealing to me. We started looking for a place to live and since we had two dogs and a cat, our options were limited. We decided not to buy a house but to rent an apartment so that we could figure out where we ultimately wanted to locate.

We finally found a tiny two-bedroom apartment that allowed pets and we rented it for six months. The apartment had a doggy door and small side yard that was perfect for our animals. Our next task was to get rid of our house in El Dorado Hills that we had lived in for seventeen years. This was no easy job because the real estate market was soft and houses in our area were not selling. We finally found a young woman who had one child, a boy, who was interested in buying it but needed to rent it while she was working through some personal problems. We rented it to her for a price that covered our mortgage payment. Now it was time for our big move to Carson City.

What a challenge that was! We were moving from a 2,400 sq. ft. house into a 600 sq. ft. apartment. We solved part of the problem by selling off a lot of the stuff that we had accumulated in nearly forty years of married life. We fixed the rest of the problem by moving only the stuff that we needed into our tiny apartment and storing the rest. On October 30, 1995, Bobbie, Tolka and Tara, (our two Norwegian Elkhounds), Charm, (our cat), and I arrived in Carson City to begin what was to become one of the happiest times in our lives.

The evening that we arrived, little kids kept showing up at our front door, "trick or treating". We told the first group of kids that Halloween was the next night but they insisted that it was that night. Bobbie and I were totally unprepared and had no candy for them. Luckily, I had a jar full of change and was able to satisfy their desires and we were not subject to any "tricks". The next day we discovered why Nevada celebrates Halloween a day early.

October 31st was the day that Nevada was admitted into the United States and all of Carson City rejoices this occasion by having parades and various exciting contests such as driving spikes into rocks etc. Consequently, Halloween arrives a day early in Nevada. Since this was our first day in Carson City, we really did not know how to get around town in order to get something to eat and to shop. The parade went up the main street, Carson Street, and we were not able to drive across town. This pissed me off and it was the first and last time that I had second thoughts about our move from Sacramento.

However, we were able to find a 7-11 on our side of Carson Street, and after some Bloody Marys and a breakfast of bacon and eggs, we felt much better.

About a year ago, our local newspaper, "The Appeal", asked the local residents what they thought about living in Carson City. This is what we wrote:

WHY WE LOVE CARSON CITY

My wife, Barbara, and I moved to Carson City six years ago from Sacramento, California. We had been coming here since the early sixties for both business and pleasure and thought Carson might be a place that we would enjoy.

Well, we love living here and daily thank God for this opportunity. What do we like about living here? What's not to like? The air is so pure, the sky is so gorgeous, the stars are so bright, and the climate is constantly changing.

I can drive to anyplace I need to go in less than five minutes and I can walk to my office in the charming Saint Charles hotel from home.

Our style is to have lunch out on a daily basis and the choice of wonderful restaurants is fabulous.

In the evening, entertainment abounds from gaming to shows to music and plays.

The local government seems dedicated and the people who live here are open and friendly.

As I said, what's not to like?

Once we had settled into our apartment I started to look for some office space for Pilot. I wanted an office in a building that had executive suites since I would be the only office staff that Pilot would have in Carson City. The only place that had such offices was the Saint Charles Hotel, one of the oldest hotels in the State of Nevada. A local businessman had purchased the hotel and converted the second floor rooms into offices. The upper floors he kept as hotel rooms. The first floor was occupied by a restaurant so the building had much the same feel to it as my old Telos office had in Old Sacramento. I rented an office that had a view of the capital building and I was in business.

I was never an employee of Pilot Computer Services until right before the acquisition of Pilot by MSXI in December of 1998. Rather than operate as a sole proprietorship, Bobbie and I formed a corporation, Silber Software Solutions, and executed a contract with Pilot on March 1st, 1996. This contract had the same basic $900.00 per month retainer as my personal contract with Pilot had, except now I would also be paid commissions on any revenue that I generated. This was a good deal for Pilot and also a good deal for me because it didn't take me too long to build the business up with the various State agencies located in Carson City. After about 18 months I had over twenty employees working for Pilot locally and Pilot was making good profits and Silber Software Solutions was collecting very nice commissions.

The three founders of Pilot were Jim O'Day, Peter Jackson, and Charles Harbour, three of the nicest guys you could ever meet, and three of the most unlikely guys ever to run a computer staffing business. Prior to forming Pilot, Jim had been one of my Telos clients when he worked for Delta Dental as Vice President of Information Technology. Charles had worked for Jim as one of his managers at Delta and since he was black, he provided the necessary ingredient for Pilot to be considered a minority owned firm. Peter was a tall, handsome fellow from Boston who used to be in the computer leasing business, and had leased computers to Jim at Delta.

After they had incorporated Pilot, Jim brought Peter and Charles to my office at Telos and introduced them to me. Since I had to have a minority firm as a subcontractor on my bids to the State and County, I gave Pilot their first break and it really paid off big time for me in the future.

Jim had suffered a heart attack while he was working for Delta and could no longer work full time. He was the money guy for Pilot and financed most of the operation. Although he could only work part time, and had no official title with Pilot, there was no question as to who was the boss. Charles was the president and his office, the corporate headquarters, was located in Concord, California. Pete was a vice president and his role was mainly in sales. Pilot also had a small office in Sacramento that was manned with a couple of incompetents whose names I can't remember.

When I first started working with Pilot, I only did so on a part-time basis to give me something to do. After a few months it became obvious to me that I would have to get more involved if Pilot was to be successful. My first clue was when it came time to re-bid the Nevada Master Services contract. The Concord office prepared the proposal and sent it up to me for delivery to the State. It was the worst piece of crap that I had ever seen. It was full of typos, misspellings, factual errors, and was totally unprofessional. I called Charles and told him that he still had a couple of days to go before the proposal was due and that he had better make the document accurate before I would submit it to the State. What he sent me the second time was much better, not perfect, but good enough to have our contract renewed.

The next thing I had to do was to convince Jim that in order to grow Pilot he would have to de-emphasize its minority status and start becoming a prime vendor to the State and County governments. Jim agreed, and since I was very well connected to both Sacramento County and the State of California, I was able to secure contracts for Pilot with these government organizations. The next thing on my agenda was to get some competent staff for the Sacramento office. The first person I hired was Renee Murray who had worked for Telos in Sacramento as both a recruiter and salesperson. The next person I brought in was Jan Arnold who was still working for Telos at that time. She had had a falling out with Melissa so it wasn't like I was raiding my old company.

Russ Waltrip, who had been Director of Information Technology for Sacramento County, retired, and I hired him to manage Pilot's Sacramento office. What a mistake that was! Jim and Russ were two strong-headed tough guys who couldn't agree on anything, and I was constantly getting in the middle of their arguments. I told Russ that I would leave Pilot before I allowed anything to interfere with our friendship. Russ, being the good guy that he is, decided to take a direct assignment with one of my clients, and that solved the problem, although to this day, Jim and Russ don't like each other.

Now I was responsible not only for Carson City, but Sacramento as well. I probably could have taken over the Concord office but that would have required Bobbie and me to relocate back to California, and that wasn't going to happen. I made Jan Arnold the manager of Sacramento and she started to hire her own staff, including my son, Patrick, who was a manager at Raley's. Pat wanted to learn the business since he had heard me talking about it his entire life. Pat quickly caught on and became a great salesman and now is the president of his own staffing company.

Back in Carson City, Bobbie and I started to look for a permanent place to live. We had decided not to live in Silver Springs and to concentrate on finding a home in Carson City. The City Treasurer was an old friend of mine and used to work for me as a programmer at Telos. He had a buddy who was a realtor who showed us some terrible looking dumps that we could not conceivably live in. We "dumped" him and found a new realtor who found us a lot on the corner of 5th and Minnesota Streets. This was a perfect location, on the edge of the Historic District, and within walking distance to my office, restaurants, and casinos. She introduced us to the builder who showed us his plans for building a duplex on this lot. We immediately purchased the duplex and the lot even though he had not started building it. This was lucky because Bobbie was able to make several changes to his plans that would make living in the place much more comfortable. We moved in sometime in August of 1996 and have no plans to move ever again.

Our duplex consists of a lovely three-bedroom, two-bath, kitchen, and great-room on each side. Both sides have a nice grassy front lawn, enclosed by a picket fence, and large patios in the rear. We built the duplex to serve both as our home and as an investment to supplement what we thought would be a rather meager retirement income.

When we decided not to move to Silver Springs, after a few false starts, we rented our property to a reliable fellow who is the service manager for our local Cadillac dealership. As a matter of fact, we bought a relatively new Seville from his shop with the proviso that if the car turned out to be a lemon he would be "out on the street." As it turned out, he was a marvelous tenant, and bought the property from us at a price that was beneficial to him as well as to Bobbie and me. His credit was not all that great, so conventional financing was not an option for him. We financed his purchase and we will have a nice income from that property, for perhaps, the rest of our lives.

The first tenant we had in our duplex was a young woman with two small children whose credit was also lousy. Bobbie and I decided to take a chance on her mainly because her children, a boy and a girl were adorable and well behaved. She proved to be a reasonably good tenant and was only late with her rent a couple of times. After about a year she left to move back to Minnesota where her ex-husband lived. She left the place spotless.

We had a few other tenants after Peggy that were OK, but about four years ago we lucked out and rented our place to Mary and Wayne who are absolutely the best tenants a landlord could dream of. Wayne works as the food and beverage manager of a local casino and Mary does not work. When Bobbie and I take our out-of-town trips she takes excellent care of our pets for us. She also pays the rent ahead of time and is absolutely delightful to have as a neighbor. Boy, were we lucky!

Although Jim had no official position in Pilot as an officer of the company, he was on the Board of Directors, and there was no question as to who was the boss. His management style, probably from growing up in the Bronx, New York, was fear and intimidation. The other side of Jim was loyalty and generosity.

Jim brought to Pilot quite a few of his old employees from his days at Delta and prior jobs. Despite some demonstrated incompetence, he would never fire them and kept them employed even while berating them. His generous nature insisted that every employee at Pilot have stock in the company, whether that person was a file clerk or an executive. When we sold Pilot to MSXI, every Pilot employee received a nice chunk of cash for his or her stock.

The interaction of Pilot's three principal owners was a sight to behold. Charles had worked for Jim for many years so he knew that Jim "was all bark and no bite." Peter, on the other hand, perceived Jim's comments as threats, and there were occasions when I thought the two of them would come to blows. Although that never happened, the relationship got so strained that Peter decided to quit Pilot and move back to Boston. Peter acted too hastily, and after he left Pilot, his financial situation deteriorated and he was forced to file for bankruptcy. That was really unfortunate as the proceeds from the sale of his stock to MSXI went to satisfy Peter's creditors and he never saw a dime for all his efforts on behalf of Pilot.

Jim decided that Pilot needed a president and because I would not move back to California, he hired one of his old buddies, Mike Rogers, to act in that capacity. Mike was a cocky, arrogant Brit., and since I was the COO, I had to report to him. Not for long!

I had decided to hire a woman that I had met to market for me in Reno and Las Vegas. Mike insisted that he wanted to interview her and make the decision as to whether or not Pilot would hire her. When I found out what Mike was up to we had a rather intense telephone conversation.

"Mike," I said. "I understand that you want to interview Cheryl when I have already decided to hire her and move her to Reno."

He responded, "You don't have the authority to hire people for new regions. That is my responsibility as president."

"Kiss my ass, Mike. I am the COO and I will make all the decisions that effect the operations of this company. If you don't like it have Jim call me and tell me that I don't have that kind of authority and Jim will have my resignation forthwith. And furthermore, Mike, I no longer report to you so don't bother calling me in the future."

I, of course, hired Cheryl and she turned out to be a huge disappointment. I had to let her go after about three months. If Mike hadn't been so uptight, I might never have hired Cheryl, but he had my Irish up.

The Sacramento and Nevada offices of Pilot were doing extremely well but the Concord office was struggling, in no small part due to Mike's management style. At any rate, Jim thought that we had probably reached the size where Pilot might be attractive to one of the sharks that were swallowing up little companies like ours.

The next character that Jim brought into the fray was Mark Dixon, an A&M (Acquisition and Merger) specialist whose company, Aquest, was located in New York City. Mark was also one of the brightest guys I have ever known. Back in the late 1980's and early 1990's there was a feeding frenzy taking place in the IT staffing industry. The big companies were gobbling up the small staffing companies, and the principals of the little companies were making fortunes. Mark tried to sell us to a huge staffing company located in Indiana but that deal fell through. The only impact that had on Bobbie and me was that we were on a steamboat cruise that included a stop in Louisville for the Kentucky Derby. After enjoying the 1998 Derby and the delightful city of Louisville, we spent two miserable nights on the steamboat. We decided to get off the boat in Paducah, Kentucky. We flew home so I could attend a meeting with our potential new owners. That deal did not materialize, but Mark put his finger on what Pilot needed to do in order to become an attractive acquisition. Our financials were very weak and Mark suggested that we hire our accountant, Paul Whalen, and have him become Pilot's Chief Financial Officer. We agreed to do so, but not without a price. Paul required a hefty salary and an equity stake in Pilot in order to abandon his accounting practice and spend full time as Pilot's CFO.

Mark had done several deals with MSXI, a billion dollar company, located in the Detroit, Michigan area. He introduced us to Roger Freidholm, the President of MSXI. Roger was a likeable fellow who understood the IT staffing business and who wanted to acquire a few more companies that were strategically located across the United States. Pilot was a good fit because MSXI, at that time, did not have any operations in northern California or Nevada. Paul Whalen had done a good job on Pilot's books and Roger was interested in buying us.

We had to send back to Michigan all of our accounts receivables, accounts payables, contracts, and personnel files so that Price Waterhouse, hired by MSXI, could conduct due diligence. After several months MSXI made an offer to buy all of the stock from the Pilot shareholders for 15 million dollars. As part of the deal I had to resign my position as president and director of Pilot and sign a seven-year non-compete agreement with MSXI. A sorry mistake on my part!

At the closing Champagne Ceremony, which took place in our attorney's office in San Francisco, Mike Rogers was prancing around stuffed up like a bantam rooster, accepting all the praise from the MSXI executives for making Pilot a worthwhile acquisition. The reality was that all of us, Jim, Charles, Peter, Paul, Mike, and I had made contributions to the success of Pilot. I can also state, unequivocally, that if I had not gotten involved with Pilot in 1990, none of this would have happened.

The deal looked good on paper, but in retrospect, we should have done a better job of negotiating; however, none of us, with the exception of Mark, had any experience in selling a company. Signing the non-compete was a terrible mistake on my part, and the agreement came back to bite me in the ass in the future.

Also, MSXI only paid one-third down, with several accounts receivable holdbacks, and the balance was to be paid over two years depending on our EBIT (earnings before income tax) numbers. This also was a serious mistake on our part as we no longer had control of our financial records. At any rate the deal closed in December of 1998 and I received a check from MSXI for $332,843.48. Not bad, considering I had joined Pilot four years previously just to give me a little something to do in Carson City. The most exciting part of the deal, I thought, was that I had another 1.5 million coming to me over the next two years. Think again, John!

Chapter Twelve
MSXI

1999 - 2002

Several years before the acquisition of Pilot took place, I got a very disturbing phone call from John Howitt, my mother's stockbroker. I had not spoken to my mother for several years and had no intention of re-establishing a relationship with her. John told me that she was in the early stages of dementia and had broken her hip after falling down on a street in New York City. I called the hospital and was told that because of her mental condition they were not going to release her and would be transferring her to the nursing home wing of the hospital. I told them not to but they insisted that she be transferred. In retrospect, I should not have interfered, but at one point earlier on, I had promised my mother that she would never be sent to a nursing home.

I explained the situation to my sister who was living in New York City. Pat did not want to deal with it because she, too, had been on the outs with our mother for many years. So Bobbie and I flew back to New York in order to solve the problem. We soon became enmeshed in the industry that feeds off the elderly. First, we met with a lawyer who had been recommended to us. She advised us on what we needed to do to get my mother released from the hospital. Next, we met with an organization that would provide twenty four-hour care for her, and any other services that she might require, such as taking her to a doctor or dentist. Now it was time to get her out of the hospital and the nightmare began.

When we went to the hospital to take my mother back to her apartment, we met with her social worker, who strongly advised us against taking her out of the hospital. We also met with the doctor in charge of her care who offered us the same advice. However, Bobbie and I were bound and determined to return her to her home where we had arranged for twenty-four hour care, beginning the next day. After several hours they agreed to release her to us, and when we first saw her she was sitting in a wheel chair and was being restrained by what looked like a straight jacket. She seemed to recognize Bobbie but she didn't have a clue as to who I was. When I asked her if she knew who I was, she replied, "Yes, you're her husband."

"Yes, but I'm also your son."

"My son? I didn't know I had two sons." I gave up.

Once out of the hospital, we removed the restraints, put her wheelchair in the trunk of the cab, put her in the back of the cab with Bobbie and that's when the fun began. The first thing she did while getting into the cab was to hit Bobbie on the ankle with her cane. Next came a tirade about how rotten the doctors and nurses in the hospital were and how they didn't realize that they were dealing with a very important person.

We got her back to the apartment without any further incidents. After feeding her and having her sign a power of attorney, so that we could pay her bills, we put her to bed for the night. Because there was only one bed in her place, Bobbie volunteered to spend the night sleeping in a chair in the living room while I returned to our hotel.

The next morning when I returned to my mother's apartment, Bobbie was a wreck. She hadn't slept all night because my mother refused to stay in bed and Bobbie had no restraints available to use. Bobbie had to hide her cane, because she was afraid of being bashed on the head by my sweet mother. We called the doctor to inquire about her bizarre behavior and found out that the hospital had neglected to give us her medication, Haldol, which kept her somewhat under control. Also, while Bobbie was wandering around the apartment that evening she discovered all kinds of cash tucked away in the bathroom, in books, in the kitchen, and all over the place. My mother would have the doorman go to the bank for her to cash checks, and then forgetting what she needed the money for, would tuck it away. God knows how much her cleaning lady and the doorman stole from her.

Finally, the Irish girls that would take care of her for the next few months arrived and Bobbie and I were free to go back home. We had made a huge mistake in taking her out of the hospital. We kept getting calls from the various women responsible for her care telling us that she was impossible and that they were going to quit. After several months of constantly replacing her caregivers, I told my sister that she had to get involved because we could not handle the situation anymore from across the country. Pat arranged to have her placed in a nursing home that specialized in Alzheimer patients. Pat got her a private room in the nursing home where she had the proper care that she could never get in her apartment. It was a very expensive place, charging over $9,000.00 a month with lots of extras to pay for. My mother had $225,000.00 in stock when she went there and when she died in November of 1995 she had nothing left because the nursing home took it all. We all did what we thought was the best for her, but it was a very sorry ending to what was probably a sad life.

The first very serious mistake that MSXI made after acquiring Pilot, was to appoint Mike Rogers as the general manager. This was done at Mark Dixon's insistence, despite all the advice to the contrary that he was given. Mike tried his hardest to eliminate Jim's control of Pilot and he might have succeeded except for the untimely death of Paul Whalen, our CFO. Paul had also been appointed as Pilot's shareholder's representative after the acquisition. With Paul out of the picture Jim became the shareholder's representative which frustrated Mike's attempt to eliminate his influence over policy.

In the months prior to the finalization of the sale of Pilot to MSXI, a transition team was created with Mike and Paul representing Pilot. Despite all the careful planning, the actual transition to MSXI ownership was dreadful. Pilot's accounting functions were transferred from Concord to Michigan. For several months MSXI failed to create invoices to the Pilot customers and when they finally started to send invoices, they were incorrect. I personally spent countless hours working with my customers trying to correct the problems that shouldn't have existed in the first place. It took MSXI over six months to get it right and even then mistakes kept occurring.

The MSXI payroll function was equally bad. We lost several subcontractors and employees because MSXI would not pay the subcontractors on a timely basis and made mistakes with our employee's fringe benefits. When we were running our own books these mistakes would not be tolerated but it seemed as if nobody at MSXI responsible for our accounting gave a damn.

After a few months Mark finally discovered that Mike was the wrong guy to run the Pilot operation and he came up with a solution which I thought was totally wrong. He wanted to bring in an outsider, Tony, to become the general manager of Pilot. I was furious about this suggestion and expressed my feelings in a memo to Jim.

Jim bought my argument and was able to dissuade Mark from bringing Tony on board. Mike saw the handwriting on the wall and resigned his position and took a job with another company. MSXI came to their senses and on October 18, 1999 appointed me to the position of general manager for Pilot Computer Service reporting to Bill Hazelton.

Bill Hazelton, although relatively new to MSXI, was put in charge of the seven IT staffing companies that MSXI had purchased. Bill was a splendid person and a knowledgeable executive. He would visit with my staff and me on a monthly basis in Sacramento where we would present him with a list of problems that we were experiencing as a result of MSXI's Accounting and Human Resources organizations. He told us that all of the recent acquisitions were experiencing similar problems and that we were not being singled out for this unacceptable behavior on the part of MSXI. We did see some improvement as a result of Bill's actions. Unfortunately, Bill could not accomplish as much as he wanted to, quit in frustration, and was replaced by another new MSXI employee, Bob Carlson.

I was put in charge of Pilot too late in 1999 to have any impact on our EBIT and the net result was that the ex-Pilot shareholders did not receive any more money from the sale of Pilot to MSXI except for the release of some of the accounts receivable holdbacks. I received about $40,000 instead of the $477,225.00 that I was expecting. We talked about protesting to the MSXI management because our lack of performance was in no small way caused by their actions. Jim's strategy, as the shareholders representative, was not to cause a fuss this year because our earn out was cumulative, and we could make it up the following year.

Being in charge of Pilot, under the pressure of the terms of the acquisition by MSXI, put me in a real conflict of interest situation. On the one hand, as a former Pilot stockholder, in order to maximize the amount of money we would receive from MSXI, I had to do everything in my power to keep costs down and profits up. On the other hand, as an MSXI executive, I had an obligation to make sound investments that would be costly in the short term but would yield higher profits for MSXI after the earn-out period was over. I made some very good business decisions that benefited both the ex-Pilot shareholders and MSXI, and I made some bad decisions that hurt the ex-Pilot shareholders. Not that it ultimately mattered, because the Pilot shareholders were not going to receive from MSXI the money they thought they were entitled to.

A couple of the really good things that I did were to hire Neal Jones and Judi Gesh who had previously worked for me at Telos. Neal came with a contract in his pocket so he was profitable from day one. Judi had excellent contacts, and it did not take her long to cash in some chips. My biggest mistake was in opening an office in Boise, Idaho. I hired the two same people that had worked for me at Telos but this time, for some unknown reason, they had a different agenda. They were spending money like crazy and accomplishing very little. After several months I decided to let them go but Bill Hazelton wanted to give them more time. I explained to him what impact this would have on our earn-out but he said, not to worry, as we would not be charged for this added time. After a few more months and an ugly termination, I closed the Boise office. When it came time for the final earn out calculations, we had to fight like hell with the MSXI executives because Bill was gone and they did not feel like honoring his commitment to me.

By the end of our second year under the ownership of MSXI, we were doing pretty well and Jim kept calculating what our earn-out was supposed to be. We recognized that we were not going to get what we had originally expected, but Jim thought we would have several million dollars to distribute to the ex-Pilot shareholders. Were we in for a surprise! According to the MSXI calculations of our earn out we were going to get a big fat nothing with the exception of the remainder of the holdback for accounts receivables. They charged us with exorbitant overhead items that were clearly not to be charged to us by our interpretation of the contract. MSXI had no intention of changing their position so the majority ex-shareholders had no choice but to hire an attorney and accountant to defend our position. After spending over $200,000.00 it became apparent to Jim and the rest of us that we did not have nearly enough resources to beat this billion-dollar corporation. Although we felt that we were wronged, we agreed to accept a settlement that was far less than we honestly thought we were entitled to. In talking to Jim recently, (Jim is a very good friend of mine currently living in Florida) we both agreed that the sale of Pilot was a good deal even for what we actually received.

When I first met Bob Carlson, he was under the impression that because of my age I was planning to retire as soon as the earn-out was completed. I had to persuade Bob that I had no plans for retiring and that I wanted to work for as long as I could be productive. He had no problem with that, because of all the companies that MSXI had acquired, Pilot was the only one that was operating profitably. As a matter of fact, sales in 2001 were 20 percent higher than sales in 2000 and profits were 64 percent greater. I believe that the reason the other companies were under-performing was that the entrepreneurs that had created these companies had taken their money and run. MSXI put in their own management with the corresponding results.

Bob Carlson, an excellent manager, was unable to accomplish

what needed to be done, became frustrated, and quit MSXI. Derek Grills, my last manager at MSXI, replaced him. Derek, because I did not believe in the changes he wanted to make, was bound and determined to get rid of me, which he did, but not without a fight.

The first thing Derek did was reorganize, combining the Engineering Technology Organization with the IT Staffing organization and naming the new group the "Human Capital Management" organization. He then appointed a national sales manager, national operations manager, and national recruiting manager. His plan was to have all the sales people report to the national sales manager, all the operations people report to the national operations manager, and all the recruiters report to the national recruiting manager. In other words, nobody would be responsible at the local level and everything would be centralized back in Michigan.

His plan for me was to put me in charge of government business on a national basis and remove me from the management of Pilot. Derek, with his national managers, came to Sacramento on August 24th, 2001 to explain the new organization to my staff and me. I thought the man was crazy and I sent him a memo, being as polite as I could under the circumstances. I told him that I did not want a staff position as the guru of government business. I also told him that since I was managing the only successful operation of the seven companies that MSXI had acquired, that I should be appointed to the position of Western Regional Manager.

I heard from Derek, that despite my August 24th memo, he was going to go forward with his plans and reorganize me out of a job. In frustration, I sent him an e-mail on September 4th, 2001, which pointed out that, "If it ain't broke, don't fix it." I also presented a proposition and challenge to him. I asked him to let me operate Pilot/MSXI in its current configuration for the year 2002 and if I did not outperform the rest of his organization by whatever measurement criteria he established, I and my staff would resign effective January 1, 2003. This is known as betting our jobs on what we could do. I told him that he could use Pilot/MSXI as one model and the rest of his organization as the other model and see which works best.

His response was: "John – interesting proposal, we will review, discuss when you visit next week. Derek"

I spoke to Derek several times on the telephone but he refused to discuss my proposal and insisted that I come back to Michigan to talk about my new role as the "government guy." I was really getting sick of the entire situation and submitted the following letter of resignation on September 19th, 2001.

September 19, 2001

Resignation

I find it inconceivable that the management of the HCM Organization did not take the trouble to respond to two different proposals that I made relative to the reorganization in process. I also find it amazing that with all my successful years in the staffing business, and my successful management of Pilot/MSXI, that my advice was not requested in order to assist in the reorganization effort.

It is unfortunate that the management changes that have occurred have forced me to leave MSXI before I was ready to, and before I wanted to. It appears that the current management wants to remove me from my position, as general manager of Pilot/MSX because their perception is that my age is detrimental to their future plans

Therefore, I am resigning my position as general manager of Pilot/MSXI. as of September 30, 2001.

Since I was required to sign a 7-year non-compete (Agreement to Preserve Corporate Opportunity) prior to the acquisition of Pilot by MSXI, and since I will not be able to work in my profession for four and a third years, I believe a severance package is appropriate. Appropriate to me would be payment though 2002 either with payroll or in a lump sum.

John K. Silberman

JOHN K. SILBERMAN

General Manager
Pilot/MSXI

His response to me was:

John, I was sorry to receive your letter of resignation and am particularly sorry that you declined to meet with me prior to tendering your resignation. As you know, I had asked that you come to Michigan and meet with me personally so that we could discuss your future with MSXI. I had intended to discuss your proposals regarding reorganization at that time and was especially looking forward to working with you and leveraging your government expertise across the HCM organization.

Your recent conduct has given me cause for concern. Specifically, I am concerned that you have made statements to your staff that are divisive and contrary to my goals for the HCM organization. I outlined those goals very clearly when I met with you and your staff in Sacramento and discussed integration and the need to brand and leverage acquired companies into an MSX Human Capital basket of products. The fact that you have presented your staff with an alternative to these integration goals before discussing such an alternative with me — even to the point of gaining consensus to proceed with your alternative plan and depart en masse if your plan failed — is inappropriate. I expect you to garner support for management goals among your staff — not counteract our goals. I now face a serious impediment to moving your group forward to create continued growth. As to your request for a severance package equal to fifteen months salary based on your Agreement to Preserve Corporate Opportunity, please note that this document was executed in conjunction with the Purchase Agreement. As a shareholder of the seller, you received substantial consideration for your execution of the Agreement to Preserve Corporate Opportunity. No further consideration for the non-compete provisions of that document will be offered. Moreover, as an at-will employee of MSXI who has voluntarily terminated his employment, you are not entitled to severance. All being said, I reluctantly accept your resignation.

Derek Grills
Sr. Vice President
Human Capital Management

Derek said a lot of things in his letter accepting my resignation that were completely untrue and on September 22, 2001, I responded:

Resignation Acceptance

Derek,

Thanks for reluctantly accepting my resignation. Actually, from the tone of your e-mail, you do not sound very reluctant.

I need to set the record straight concerning your comments to me. You stated that I made comments to my staff that are "divisive and contrary" to your goals for the HCM organization The fact of the matter is that I presented this proposal to you by e-mail on September 4th and you acknowledged it by e-mail on the same date by saying "Interesting proposal, we will review/ discuss when you visit next week." How come it was interesting then and now it is divisive and contrary? I told my staff that they should be proud of their accomplishments and should continue to bring success to the HCM organization. On our August 24th meeting I reported to you with all of my staff present that we were set for a 30 percent growth in revenue and a 230 percent growth in margin over year 2000. I told you that the "success of this operation is due to the team effort by the people sitting in this room. We operate as a team and achieve as a team."

You stated that you were especially looking forward to working with me and leveraging my government expertise across the HCM organization. I told you in person on August 24th that I was not interested in a staff position working in that capacity. On August 27th, I told you that I was extremely flattered by your offer, Derek, of working directly for you as the guru of government business but I think it would be a misuse of my talent, etc. It is obvious that by your actions and your words your intent was to reorganize me out of the job in which I achieved great success for MSXI. Why would you do that?

You stated, "You have presented your staff with an alternative to these integration goals before discussing such an alternative with me." I presented my proposal to you on September 4th. I find it interesting that you make these comments to me after my resignation and not before. What is your purpose?

You go on to say, "Even to the point of gaining consensus to proceed with your alternate plan and depart en masse if your plan failed — is inappropriate." What I said was that I would bet my job on what I could do for you and MSXI and that my staff would bet their jobs on what we could achieve for you. That was a positive statement of our confidence in our ability to achieve success and was not a threat to resign en masse.

You stated, "I now face a serious impediment to moving your group forward to create continuous growth." In my letter to my managers announcing my resignation, I stated, "You are all very talented people and I know that Pilot/MSXI will continue to be successful in the future through your dedication and knowledge of the business." Any failure to achieve growth will be your failure, Derek, not mine.

Your denial of my request for an appropriate severance package is totally without merit and I am not surprised at your lack of understanding.

On September 24th, Derek requested a meeting with me to discuss the entire situation.

We established a meeting in Sacramento on October 8th, 2001.

After spending several hours with my staff and me, Derek said, "Evidently you are the glue that holds this organization together." Jan and the rest of my staff apparently told him that without me, he could not count on them staying for any appreciable length of time. Derek and I came to a twelve-point agreement and I thought that I had won the battle hands down. Was I ever wrong! The main part of the agreement was that I was to remain in charge of Pilot indefinitely.

Pilot/MSXI continued to grow under my leadership and I even got a $7,500.00 increase in salary on October 1st, 2001. What I hadn't realized was that Derek, behind my back, was soliciting the loyalty of my key managers, like Jan, to support his new organization structure even though I had told him on many occasions that it was doomed to failure. Derek was determined to do it his way and I found out that he had no intention of honoring his October 8th agreement with me. "John to remain in charge of this group indefinitely, reporting directly to Derek." The new definition of "indefinitely" was four months, for that is how long it took him to undermine me with my staff and get rid of me. I was tired of fighting the war so we reached a new agreement on February 25th 2002, which essentially removed me from my management of Pilot and made me a senior consultant to the Northwest Region of MSXI.

I wondered how long it would take for Derek to breach this contract. I didn't have to wait long as I received the following letter from him on September 27th, 2002:

Dear John:

This letter is to confirm our discussion today regarding your employment separation from MSX International. Our current business performance requires that we take action to reduce our operating costs and reorganize specific operations. With regret, I must inform you that your position is being eliminated effective September 30, 2002.

Sincerely,

(Signed)

Derek Grills
Senior Vice President
Human Capital Management Services

I have always believed that "what goes around, comes around" and in 2003 Derek was let go by MSXI and was replaced by Mr. Payne who put the organization back the way I had recommended all along. Jan now has my old job as Western Regional Manager. Jan for my 70th birthday tribute wrote:

"All right, all right. Enough of that. I was told I HAD to say something nice (your kids asked because they said you are getting old and we should try to be nice to you). So, here's the truth if you can stand it (well, at your age, you better sit down). Without a doubt you have been one of the most influential people in my life. There's my father, my mother and you. You have been an excellent mentor and I know my parents hold you in high regard in helping to raise me after I left the nest (btw, they blame you for the three marriages!). Your eternal optimism, which I know is influenced by your talented and very intelligent wife (it's true that it IS the woman who makes the man), has always been a true delight. As a friend, a mentor and practically a family member (unless the dock burns down and you go broke), I have always treasured my relationship with you and look forward to many fabulous years ahead (even if I do have to spend those years pushing your wheelchair). Sorry, it's just too hard for me to be really, genuinely kind for any length of time. You, of all people, can understand that!"

What I didn't know was that Jan meant "pushing" me out the

door! And so this phase in my life came to an end. Whether or not there will be additional chapters remains to be seen. I kind of suspect that there might be one or two "rabbits" left to be pulled out of the hat, especially when my non-compete comes to an end. I have always been a lucky kind of guy, and when the next opportunity comes around, I will be prepared for it.